Warni[ng]

Attempted [Murd]er

Exposed

God's Warning To All Americans Through A Dream

By Dr. Daniel Daves

We're at Def con 1

"An historic world-changing event is about to crush the U.S. economy and stock market." - Martin Weiss

"Progressives are leading us to fascism. Progressivism is a cancer in America!" – Glenn Beck

"The main obstacle to a stable and just world order is the United States." - George Soros

Talking of the Weather Underground, "They estimated that they would have to eliminate 25 million people in U.S. re-education centers. And when I say eliminate, I mean 'kill' 25 million people." - Larry Grathwohl, FBI Undercover Agent

Communism: A system of government under which there is no private industry and (in some forms) no private property, most things being state-owned.

Communist: A person who believes in communism. He is a Communist; a Communist leader.

Dr. Daniel Daves

Dr. Daniel Daves is "The Giant Tracker™" and is involved in business development, education, and international philanthropic works. He speaks internationally as an author and professional, helping organizations and leaders to break the negative cycles of poverty, and to align correctly with God's miraculous rhythmic cycles of life, investment, and growth. He trains students how to successfully track the secret financial movements of markets, industries, businesses and governments. Dr. Daves has a Masters degree in Missiology, a D.Min and a PhD in Christian Administration from Logos Christian College & Graduate School, Jacksonville, FL. He has 32+ years of ministry and business experience in America and on the mission field. He is married to his wife Tracy of 24 years and they have two wonderful children, Ariel & Danny.

Published By:

Mighty Eagle Publishing

P.O. Box 179, Mansfield, TX 76063

Email: info@mightyeagle.com

Web Sites: **www.mightyeagle.com   www.doctordanieldaves.com**

Table Of Contents

WARNING! Warning America! Attempted Hostile Take Over Exposed

Copyright © 2012 by Mighty Eagle Publishing

ISBN # Paperback 0-9763521-2-9   Kindle 0-9765321-1-2   iTunes 0-9763521-3-6

Published : Mighty Eagle Publishing, Dallas, TX, U.S.A.   www.mightyeagle.com

*Unless otherwise indicated, all scripture quotations are taken from the King James and New International Versions of the Bible.

**All 'communism" quotes found at www.brainyquote.com.

***All "Communism definitions found at www.thefreedictionary.com.

NOTICE & DISCLAIMER:

Dedication

This book is dedicated to the author of the dream, my Lord Jesus Christ. Without His life, power and directional light for my steps, I would not be alive today, nor would I be at peace and accomplishing kingdom tasks of eternal value. I thank God for sending His Son to die on the horrible cross of Calvary for a mark missing sinner like me. *(That cross was meant for me, yet He took it in my stead.)* And I thank God for raising His Son back to life on the third day so that I also might be raised together with Him to a new life. How great is your love, that you loved such an enemy as I, and that you are willing to share your fore-knowledge of future events through dreams which I can understand.

Dr. Daniel Daves, PhD

Warning America! Attempted Hostile Take Over Exposed

God's Warning To All Americans Through A Dream

Preface

History continually repeats itself during the course of cyclical human living. There are times when men turn from their Creator and all they have known to be true, and begin to develop alternative ideas of living, governing, wealth creation and lifestyle alterations. These alternatives are very dangerous to mankind because they stray from the confines of truth and life, and begin to encroach on others to make them less free, less prosperous and less productive. Unchecked, these alternative behaviors result in communistic styled oppression of those who wish to live freely. The results are far reaching. The impact on human souls can leave scars for generations, and the destructive forces unleashed are none less than satanic. It is absolutely true that "off the path" alternative lifestyles and thought pushed by the governing elite are the opening to hell's abyss, death and the grave for multitudes. One hundred million souls perished as a result of communistic alternative beliefs in the 20th century. How many will perish during our watch?

When alternative realities become oppressive and overwhelming in their attempt to erase history in the minds of the people, move ancient boundary stones, re-write timeless truth and enslave masses, God Himself will begin to send warnings. Sometimes He will send a series of dreams and dreamers who will send strong warning to all who can and will hear. I believe that we are standing in the day where God is sending dreams, visions and warnings to an obstinate mankind who has clearly been blinded and deafened by various noises coming from the alternative abyss. Times are critical. Billions of lives are in the valley of decision and there is a heightened risk of many perishing or falling into slavery. Will mankind heed the warnings that God is sending? Only the future will tell. However, if "you" are one who heeds the warnings, you will be moved under God's almighty wings of care and protection, safe from harm, slavery and death. Make no mistake about it. If you heed the warning, you will be making proactive movements. But to not make movements will give you no divine protection. Warnings come to move people. A person who has been warned cannot in good conscious stand still. God's warnings always require people to move by faith. Moving by faith will move you into the secret place of God's divine care and protection.

We have arrived at humanities tipping point, the end of the old, the beginning of the new, and an epic battle between powerful forces for control of the future. This is not a season of comfort, but a time to awaken, arise, become educated and be ready to move into new dimensions, new paradigms and new doors of opportunity. Let go of the old in order to embrace the new. The new will actually be more safe and prosperous for you, your family and future. And as you prepare for the new, fully understand the enemy of Communism which is sitting at the door and waiting for one last opportunity to pounce upon what's left of free America.

This enemy comes with a twist. While the foundation is communistic in nature, today's enemy is taking on a multi-headed, multi-crowned beast with the united powers of Communism, Fascism, Progressivism, Socialism, Totalitarianism, Elitism, Islam, and other movements in order to seize control of a new "One World Order".

Rev. 13:1 And I stood upon the sand of the sea, and saw a beast rise up out of the sea, having seven heads and ten horns, and upon his horns ten crowns, and upon his heads the name of blasphemy.

While these blasphemers arise to take their stand against truth, liberty, justice and freedom, the Bible declares that they will be overcome, destroyed and sent to perdition.

Revelation 17:14 These shall make war with the Lamb, and the Lamb shall overcome them: for he is Lord of lords, and King of kings: and they that are with him are called, and chosen, and faithful.

This book is a warning for the called, chosen and faithful. I will discuss ways to protect yourself, your family, faith, finances and future in later chapters. Remember that God will not give shocking information without providing direction to keep you on the correct path. The information in this book will not only reveal the probable future, but it will help you make necessary preparations for that future. May God grant you success to navigate through the perilous times ahead.

Chapter 1

The Dreamer

----

com·mu·nism:

A theoretical economic system characterized by the collective ownership of property and by the organization of labor for the common advantage of all members.

(All "Communism definitions found at www.thefreedictionary.com.)

Communism has never come to power in a country that was not disrupted by war or corruption, or both.

– John F. Kennedy

(All 'communism" quotes found at www.brainyquote.com.)

I am a dreamer. I say this because I have had a few dreams during my lifetime which have proven to be true. I have been a born again Christian since I was 18 years old, and I entered into ministry at 21 years old, including youth ministry, evangelistic ministry and eventually pastoring in churches over a 20 year period. I then moved into missions work and business endeavors. While in the ministry, I have spoken at various leadership conferences, encouraged church leaders across the globe, held positions as an overseer in churches, and I have been under continual spiritual leadership authority within the church structure. I have also started, built and sold various businesses over the decades while being in ministry. I have a spiritual father and pastor whom I've been submitted to since 1986. I tell you this because I understand the requirements and principles of authority and leadership. People who walk in leadership, authority and wisdom want to know the historical track record of a person, their character, and their long term fruit which has been produced (if any).

1 Tim 5:22 (NIV) 22 Do not be hasty in the laying on of hands, and do not share in the sins of others. Keep yourself pure.

I have had dreams in my life that proved to be very directional and powerful in pointing my attention and efforts into a particular area. Without fail, these dreams have been proven accurate in detail and direction. It's with this historical foundation of success, along with my continued immersion in the Word of God, the Holy Bible, and a strong attempt to continually develop a strong relationship with my God and Savior, the Lord Jesus Christ, that I believe that my dreams come from God as a form of directional knowledge. However, I say with humility that it is possible that my dreams are in error and false. I acknowledge that. But I can honestly say before God that I absolutely believe them to be true, with 100% willingness to invest all I have into the direction of these dreams.

My initial dream of 2008 has constantly unfolded and proven to be true. Only a few key announcements and shifts need to happen in order to completely finalize the dream. These upcoming announcements will be the most important shifting events that will re-shape and finalize the total transformation of America and will change the world forever. There is a second dream that I had in 2009 which gives a full and clear picture of "the end". This book is about those dreams, their interpretations, and how you can position yourself to protect your family, future and faith against the horrible future that these dreams announce for many.

The first dream that came to me in 2008 was not like the old "pizza" dream, or the senseless dreams that are easy to forget within hours of waking up. This dream has been imprinted into my mind as a real, fully detailed memory. I received the dream as if I were actually physically present inside the dream and it was real to me in a literal sense. This dream, and another similar dream that I had later that year, are the two dreams that I am going to discuss in this book.

I realize that the gift of the dreamer is a sacred one. This gift is desired by many, but unfortunately only released into some. I joke around sometimes that my dreams must be a sign of my age, because I never had a dream until I was 40 years old.

Joel 2:28 (KJV) 28 And it shall come to pass afterward, that I will pour out my spirit upon all flesh; and your sons and your daughters shall prophesy, your old men shall dream dreams, your young men shall see visions.

I have always been a visionary and had strong vision for the future which has driven my life, business affairs, and ministry. Maybe the dreams come to me because I'm getting older. Regardless, I want to honor God who gives the gift of dreams, and I honor the dreams I've been given as holy and sacred. For some reason, God saw fit to pierce into a dimension of my life and reveal present and future events for a very powerful reason. I believe that God wants to help people, protect the innocent, and give warning and direction to those who are crying out for God's wisdom. Therefore, I have a commitment to share what I have received, with hopes that those who have ears to hear and eyes to see, will receive the message from God's heart to yours.

Of course, I run the risk of being wrong. And if I am, I will be known in the future as the crazy guy who had the dreams that didn't come to pass. I accept that possibility with humility and fear in the Lord. However, I would not want to keep quiet and risk having innocent blood on my hands. Rather, as a watchman on the wall, I am constrained to shout loudly what I have seen and heard in hopes that some will hear and be saved from future potential destruction.

Ezek 33:6 (NIV) **6** *But if the watchman sees the sword coming and does not blow the trumpet to warn the people and the sword comes and takes the life of one of them, that man will be taken away because of his sin, but I will hold the watchman accountable for his blood.*

I have prepared and set the direction of my family, faith, finances, and future in alignment with the dreams I had in 2008. The direction I took has proven to be correct in accordance with the dreams. I'm thankful that God was gracious enough to give me insight, foresight and H.S.I. (Holy Spirit Intelligence) into the future so that I might prepare and help others to also prepare.

Chapter 2

The First Dream – Spring 2008

----

com·mu·nism:

A stem of government in which the state plans and controls the economy and a single, often authoritarian party holds power, claiming to make progress toward a higher social order in which all goods are equally shared by the people.

"One strength of the communist system of the East is that it has some of the character of a religion and inspires the same emotions of a religion."

- Albert Einstein

It was a normal week in Spring 2008. I had spent the week preparing for a financial conference that I would be speaking at in Poplar Bluff, MO. As I went to bed the night before, I knew that I would be getting up early in Dallas, TX to pack and hitting the road for a 10+ hour drive where I needed to arrive before 6 PM that night.

Early in the morning, at around 4 AM, I had a powerful, life changing dream. I believe that it was absolutely from God. It was so real, lifelike, powerful, and convincing. It took me by surprise and the things I saw and heard in this dream were shocking and hard to grasp at the moment I was seeing and hearing them. However, through the coming weeks I would try to assimilate the dream and get a solid interpretation of what this dream "really" meant. As time moved forward, this dream would begin to unfold before my very eyes through announcements made on national and international news channels and as international events unfolded. I fully realized that the dream meant exactly what was spoken to me in the dream, and that deep code breaking interpretation was not needed. Therefore, I began making preparations for the culmination of the dream and what the future of America would look like up to, during, and after the public announcements, which I heard in the dream. These shocking announcements that I heard would soon be made publicly to the rest of the world. But before that time came, I had the distinct opportunity to hear the announcements in the dream before anyone else would hear them on earth.

And now for the dream exactly how it came to me early in the morning. I would then awaken suddenly, and begin to write the dream down on paper.

DREAM: SCENE 1

I was standing in what seemed to be the downtown Dallas, TX area along with multitudes of people. Everyone was standing and waiting for an announcement of some kind. I had a local friend standing beside me, and our two boys were playing together off to the side, over by the street. There was no traffic, as all the cars were parked. Everything was at a standstill and all the people were calm and quiet. I noticed big screens up on many of the large buildings and I sensed that a big announcement was going to be made. Then suddenly, a man who looked like a government official appeared on the big screens and began to make an announcement. He said:

"Ladies and gentlemen, I have an announcement to make. America as

you have known it has ceased to exist. All property lines have been dissolved, and the U.S. Dollar is worthless."

When the people heard this announcement, they began to panic. I felt a deep concern inside my being as I stood and watched the people begin to frantically run. They ran to their cars and ran down the sidewalks. They

all seemed to be headed in a West direction in sheer panic. I suddenly realized that our boys were in deep trouble as a frantic motorist jumped in his car and tore out of its parking place to head West. I ran over and grabbed both boys, pulling them out of the curb side area of the street, as the motorist shot past them. He would have hit and probably maimed or killed them if I hadn't gotten to them in time. I was relieved to know that the boys were safe. The multitudes continued to panic and head West. There was mayhem and confusion everywhere. I was very concerned for their safety and well being. I had clear insight inside the dream and I knew that the people were heading West.

This was the end of scene one. I would then be suddenly transported to scene two of the dream.

Dream: Scene 2

I was suddenly standing at a gas station/convenience store. This convenience store looked a little different than the typical convenience store. It had a high fence attached off to the side of it with barbed wire across the top. Inside the fence were tractors, power equipment, lawn mowers, chain saws and all kinds of different items that clearly had been recently traded. I was standing beside an Indian man who was clearly the owner or manager of the convenience store. Frantic people were pulling their vehicles up to the fuel pumps and were buying gas. My intuition told me that they were heading "WEST"?. Then an SUV pulled up with an open trailer in back. An entire family was in the vehicle and they all looked worried. They had thrown all of their belongings in the trailer and strapped items on top of the vehicle. The father jumped out of the SUV and came up to the man. He said, "I need to get a tank full of gas." and he pulled out his billfold to pull out some U.S. Dollars. The store manager said, "I don't take U.S. Dollars." The father looked concerned and asked, "What do you take then?" The manager asked, "Well, what do you have?" The father and the manager both walked over to the trailer and started looking through it, to find something of value that could be traded for a tank of gas. The store manager clearly was going to choose what he wanted in order to allow the frantic man to get some gas.

This was the end of the dream, scene two.

Dream: Scene 3

Immediately, I was standing in a very modern war room which had video screens everywhere on the wall. These screens were showing scenes from different places around the world, modern world events, etc. In the

17

middle of the room was President George W. Bush II, who was nearing the end of his presidency. He was surrounded by counselors and advisers. Many of them had clipboards and they were attempting to advise him of important issues. He had his hands up in the air as if to say, "I don't want to hear any more! I'm tired and worn out!"

I was standing beside a large man who looked like a secret service agent. He began to speak to me saying, "The president has fought a long, hard

battle and is very tired." I responded, "Yeah, I can see that." He said, "He has been fighting a very powerful enemy. Do you know who that enemy is?" I thought of all the enemies that it could be, Al Qaeda, Islam, and some of the internal enemies that I knew were harming the foundations of America. But then I said, "Socialism?" He responded with a stern voice, "Communism!".

At that time the dream ended, and I woke up sitting straight up in my bed. I didn't know for sure if my new conscience state was real, or if the dream was real. The dream had seemed so real as if I were literally there. It took me a minute to realize that I had just received a very powerful dream from God. I then got up, jotted down notes on the dream, then began to pack my bags and prepared to drive towards a financial conference in Poplar Bluff, MO.

This was the dream in its entirety. The interpretation that I've chewed on, sought out, considered and meditated on - is profound and ever-unfolding in my life. It has changed me, changed my direction, and literally changed the future of my family forever. As the years progress, different news events unfold, laws are changing, politicians make their moves, and the dream and its definitions become clearer. Many people have indicated that they believe the dream is from God. I concur.

Chapter 3

Interpretation of the First Dream, Scene 1a –
As I presently understand

----

com·mu·nism:

The Marxist-Leninist version of Communist doctrine that advocates the overthrow of capitalism by the revolution of the proletariat.

Communism is not love. Communism is a hammer which we use to crush the enemy.

- Mao Tse-Tung

The dream I had *is continually unfolding, and as it becomes real in the natural world, it opens greater understanding of things still to come. My personal interpretation of this dream is an expanding "work in progress", and it seems to be like the layers of an onion. The deeper you peel it, the better it gets. I welcome you to interpret the dream as you see fit. It's possible that you will see things that I have overlooked or could not understand. Please be my guest at interpreting the dream as you see it.*

"America as you have known it has ceased to exist."

I was standing with my friend and our sons in a large city among a huge crowd of people. This tells me that the announcement that is to come publicly is going to affect a very large group or a body of people in America, possibly the entire nation. And anything that affects America will undoubtedly make an impact on the entire world.

My son was in the dream along with my friend's son. I believe that this means that not only will the upcoming announcement affect myself, my friends, family, and nation, but also our next generation that is currently under our care. Because of the fearful reactions of those who are in authority and driving frantically when they hear the upcoming announcement, I believe our next generation will be in deep danger of being run over or aborted because of the darkened, fearful, reactionary decisions of the current driving crowd. In the dream when the fearful, reactionary man jumped in his car and drove forward with no concern for the children in front of him, I believe this indicates that many people will have no concern for the next generation when they make reactionary decisions to protect and preserve themselves. This will be a very dangerous season for the upcoming generation. I believe that God wants you and I to be protectors of the next generation and to help grab young people everywhere, dragging them from the path of a fearful, selfish, unreliable, abusive and undiscerning generation who may be making wrong reactionary decisions in their time of fear and panic.

Prov 13:22 (NIV) A good man leaves an inheritance for his children's children, but a sinner's wealth is stored up for the righteous.

I believe that God calls good men everywhere to plan for their grand children's future and to prepare an inheritance. God is the ultimate of good men, who looked into our needy future and provided His Son, the

21

Savior of mankind, to die for our sins, to raise us up together with Him, and to give us an eternal inheritance which includes a plan for prosperity and success on the earth. Yet, those who lead America have been ruthless towards our future generations and their success. We have laws that allow the convenient murder of a child in the sacred womb of his/her own mother (53+ million children so far and counting!). Our leaders have adopted the doctrines of debt which have enslaved every American and the U.S. Government. Each American owes a debt we cannot pay, and a typical American family of 4 will end up owing over $500,000 in unpaid debt in the near future. America has bankrupted herself and given her children's future to powerful world bankers who will take pleasure in seizing ownership of the inheritance that originally belonged to our children. Why? Because we have served false gods, giving in to the temptations of our flesh, to enjoy life now with the promise to pay deep into our future. Government debt is over $200 Trillion in unfunded promises. Consumer debt stands at $16 Trillion as of 2012. Unforgivable college debt is over $1 Trillion, and America's credit card debt is nearing $1 Trillion. Who will end up paying this bill? Our grandchildren will pay it, and they will hate this illicit generation who aborted their future so that we could "have our cake and eat it too" at their expense!

Quotation: "If the American people ever allow private banks to control the issue of their currency, first by inflation, then by deflation, the banks and corporations that will grow up around them will deprive the people of all property until their children wake up homeless on the continent their Fathers conquered...I believe that banking institutions are more dangerous to our liberties than standing armies... The issuing power should be taken from the banks and restored to the people, to whom it properly belongs." - Thomas Jefferson

I believe that the three part announcement which came from the governing official in the dream are three things that have already happened in secret planning rooms, and which are set in stone as far as the global driving elitist agenda is concerned. Most people don't realize that these three statements have already been settled behind closed doors among world leaders. That's why the people will be so fearful when they figure it out all at once. I don't believe that these three announcements can be changed, although I may be wrong. I recognize that it's always possible for an intercessor to activate the hand of God to stop anything. Even the sun stood still for Joshua for a day during a battle due to intercession in the Old Testament. However, I think that these three issues are solid and can be banked on. I have been studying dreams. It's my understanding from dream interpreters, that when a government official speaks from a position of power in that dream, this gives a strong case that the statements are "set in stone".

There is power for you and I as we know this dream in advance. This fore knowledge can help us understand that these three announcements are completed, finished and set in stone. We can set a course of protection, provision, and proactive planning which will be fueled by the public announcement itself. If you and I take action and set a new course in accordance with the dream, we will not be harmed by fearful reaction that will sweep the masses into a full throttled, run of mayhem towards the West. I encourage you to consider the impact of the three statements upon America and the world, and set a course that protects you, your family, your job, business, and church now. I believe that time is short.

I believe that you should realistically consider the massive impact of the three government statements. Do a spiritual survey of America, your life, and everything that you've ever known to be true. Take notes. Try to wrap your mind around the fact that your old America is gone. Try to grasp the reality that every property line and boundary you've ever known is now dissolved. Try to understand the upheaval and fear that can come upon people when they realize that their home is no longer theirs, that the rule of law and the constitution have been destroyed in America, and that the state has now made a bid to own everything that once belonged to the citizens. Once you can wrap your mind around these announcements and the new realities that are coming, you can start getting into position in favor of the three statements, rather than being fearful and reactionary when the statements are made public. We will discuss this positive positioning later in the book.

But let me remind you, accepting and trying to wrap your mind around these three statements is not easy. This is especially true when everything looks one way in the natural, yet you're being challenged to look into a very different future.

From the point that I had the dream, it took me four months to mourn the loss of my nation as I have known it. I felt like a person clinging to the casket of my dear loved one, holding on and not wanting it to go into the ground. America as I have known her has ceased to exist. She died under my watch and care. My grief was almost unbearable. To this day I still hurt for old America. If I could change her future, I'd certainly do it.

However, I realize that I must stand up with what I know and help others to prepare for a very different future which many of us have not been preparing for.

Please remember that "true" America still lives inside the hearts of patriots and freedom lovers who live an oath to defend the constitution from enemies both foreign and domestic. So while America "as we have known it" has ceased to exist, there is a "true" America that will rise up again, which can never be extinguished or destroyed.

I believe that there are some parts of America that must die according to God's plan. The America that I have always known but didn't necessarily understand had a lot of evil that must be judged and removed. I was almost totally ignorant of many of these evils until I had the dream. I then began to pursue the interpretation of the dream, and my eyes were opened to many evils and frauds that America must be cleansed from.

We live in an America which is content with the murderous destruction of 53+ million innocent babies, aborted and thrown at the feet of Jesus without even a care from a large portion of America's citizens. Did Americans wake up this (and every) morning with the heart felt pain of babies being murdered under our watch? More than likely "no". We Americans have become calloused and hardened to this murderous spirit which has been invited to live in America by murderous anti-Christ law makers.

Run away scientists have now concluded that a child as young as two years old has no true value on the earth because we cannot tell whether the child will be autistic, smart, or productive in the world. Therefore, a segment of science has given the authorization to eliminate and abort children up to two years old because their value as a human being cannot be determined.

Will this murderous, destructive, terrorist spirit be appeased by destroying life only in the womb? No. Rather, this spirit seeks to destroy children just as Herod and Pharaoh of the Old Testament did. This spirit wants to destroy the elderly, Jews, Christians, fathers, sons, families and anything else that represents God and His wonderful life-filled plans for mankind. Rest assured, there will be a standoff between this murderous spirit and the armies of Heaven! This spirit and anyone connected to it shall be destroyed by the fires of Heaven.

American corporatism and fascism has adopted and legalized massive anti-Christ behavior including genetic modification of foods, corporate take over of farms, lands and industries, and government take over of economies such as banking, automotive and medical. More take overs are in the works in a communistic styled Marxist/Stalinist/satanic mentality which cares not about God, honor, life, liberty and the pursuit of happiness.

America suffers from Pharaohistic over-taxation, destructive anti-biblical government policies, and enslavement of the masses. The removal of "honor" from our founding fathers, the constitution, bill of rights, and the family unit cannot pass through the authorizations and approval of God in Heaven.

Many of our government and corporate elitist leaders are absolutely dedicated as "Sons of Belial" and are actual, knowing and committed Satan worshippers, bent on destructive, illegal, fraudulent, lying behavior. They hinder peace and start divisive wars around the world, while making huge financial profits in doing so. These corrupted evils, and more, will be tried by fire and will be removed by God Himself, and the truth will come and replace the false.

This is the America which will eventually cease to exist, in my personal opinion. These illicit systems, policies, laws, procedures along with the officials who create them will pass through the fires of God, and will burn in the heat of His fury and wrath. He is commanding them to, "Let My People Go!" This is not a request. Just as God destroyed Pharaoh's economy and eventually dealt with his future by destroying Pharaoh's son, so God is dealing with the "economies" of the world, and will also deal with the future of the world bankers and elitists who hold the people in slavery.

"America as you've known it has ceased to exist." The good old days of baseball, hotdogs, apple pie and Chevrolet are gone. We are now a melting pot of many cultures, many religions (some very aggressive) and many ideas of how to govern America. These are all working hard to bring their own versions of a new world order, various forms of previously failed government structures, socialism, communism, dictatorial rule, police state, fascism and many more ideas and agendas. The freedoms that Americans previously enjoyed have rapidly disappeared as we have become a nation which is fundamentally changing in every sense of the word. Those who have now seized control of America are changing her laws, policies, codes, direction and structure while destroying the fundamental foundations of the country. The constitution has been absolutely shredded, openly and blatantly neglected on purpose and by "their" design. Our founding fathers would have already met in the parks with revolution in their "eyes of fire" if they were alive today. Yet the vast majority of Americans sleep, trust, and believe for false "hope and change", walking under strong delusion and deception, swaying back and forth like a drunken man, alienated from the true hope of God through the glorious gospel and the truth of God's Holy Bible.

2 Thess 2:9-12 (NIV) The coming of the lawless one will be in accordance with the work of Satan displayed in all kinds of counterfeit miracles, signs and wonders, and in every sort of evil that deceives those who are perishing. They perish because they refused to love the truth and so be saved. For this reason God sends them a powerful delusion so that they will believe the lie and so that all will be condemned who have not believed the truth but have delighted in wickedness.

When a person or nation leaves God and their founding principles, beliefs and legal documents, when they move ancient boundary stones and strive to change the fundamentals of the constitution, then the very foundations of the nation will shake, shudder and ultimately collapse if not quickly repaired. In my humble opinion, this is where America stands today. The issues are deep and complex, but they revolve around the simplicity of leaving our roots of freedom, liberty and justice "for all" in hopes of some better governing model, or at least one with more control over the people.

Prov 22:28 (NIV) Do not move an ancient boundary stone
set up by your forefathers.

The America that I knew and remember seemed to be free. It was a nation that seemed to be filled with capitalism (*the right to own land and do what you want on it without being bothered or dictated*). However, unknown to me the seeds of destructive change had been planted in America 100 years ago with the illegal, unconstitutional creation of the world banker owned Federal Reserve and the I.RS. Since then, America has suffered through depression after recession, and a 96% devaluation of the U.S. Dollar currency, high taxes, and going off of the gold standard after a better "Doctrine Of Debt" theology. America has been plagued, wearied and worn down by the powers of freedom and liberty. Because we have left our moral obligation to the U.S. Constitution, we have become morally bankrupt as a nation. Our moral failures have alienated us from the power and life of God, and we have become a nation with the "form of godliness" which is void of the powers of success. Our moral bankruptcy has infected our financial capacity to prosper, because we have blinded ourselves and lost our moral strength as a great and mighty nation.

2 Tim 3:1-9 (NIV) But mark this: There will be terrible times in the last days. People will be lovers of themselves, lovers of money, boastful, proud, abusive, disobedient to their parents, ungrateful, unholy, without love, unforgiving, slanderous, without self-control, brutal, not lovers of the good, treacherous, rash, conceited, lovers of pleasure rather than lovers of God-- having a form of godliness but denying its power. Have

29

nothing to do with them. They are the kind who worm their way into homes and gain control over weak-willed women, who are loaded down with sins and are swayed by all kinds of evil desires, always learning but never able to acknowledge the truth. Just as Jannes and Jambres opposed Moses, so also these men oppose the truth--men of depraved minds, who, as far as the faith is concerned, are rejected. But they will not get very far because, as in the case of those men, their folly will be clear to everyone.

Those days of freedom are gone, possibly forever in America. Most nations don't recover from moral bankruptcy. America will most likely never return without a massive, bloody, dirty, horrible revolution and replacement of the current system, establishment, and government as it stands today. Those who hate your personal liberties, freedoms and the "American Way" will not go down easily or without a fight. They are willing to lay down their lives for their beliefs in socialism, communism, fascism, and destruction of freedom, liberty and an environment of maximum multiplication. They don't like your fundamentals of freedom and liberty, therefore they want to fundamentally transform your nation. They are also willing to take your life, liberty, and freedom in order to propel their beliefs. If you are in their way and they are in power, they would consider removing you from the planet to further their vision. They sense no moral, legal or ethical obligation to you as a person, an individual, or a sovereign citizen of the United States. Only the "collective" counts. In their minds, their vision trumps your right to freedom and liberty. The atmosphere is toxic and the times are dangerous for all of us.

The old American system is broken, virally infected and in need of massive overhaul and repair. It has been hijacked by many opposing viewpoints and it cannot stand as long as there is division. There is a strong need for unity towards freedom and liberty if the American system will ever work again in the future. Along with unity of "we the people" will be a requirement to replace most all of those positions who are currently in power. The far left leaning beliefs and ideals of a non-rooted, always shifting and changing, emotionally led liberals must be neutralized if freedom is to return. This will not happen until millions of demoralized, ungrounded Americans change their minds, moral beliefs and opinions. This must come from a revolution of spirit, mind and belief – otherwise known as a great awakening or raising up of "believers" in truth, righteousness and Godly principles. If there was ever a time when the world needed a spiritual revolution and mass turning of the people back to Jehovah God and the freedoms that He offers, this is that time!

Hosea 6:1-3 (KJV) Come, and let us return unto the Lord: for he hath torn, and he will heal us; he hath smitten, and he will bind us up. After two days will he revive us: in the third day he will raise us up, and we shall live in his sight. Then shall we know, if we follow on to know the Lord: his going forth is prepared as the morning; and he shall come unto us as the rain, as the latter and former rain unto the earth.

What does a nation divided against itself look like? Look at America today. Politically polarized parties are at opposite extremes. The Democratic Party has been hijacked by the Marxist/Communist party just as Karl Marx said needed to happen in the Communist Manifesto. Many

Democrats are divided because they've never seen their party so far left before and they are very uncomfortable.

"I believe there is about 78 to 81 members of the Democratic Party that are members of the Communist Party."

- Rep. Allen West, 2012

The Republican Party is deeply divided among conservative right and liberal Republicans who love to use political power to prosper. Many have left their parties and are embracing constitutional republic candidates like Ron Paul who promise a return to American values. America stands on the brink of a full blown race war with racially charged language, hatred, and fueled anger.

A nation divided against itself cannot stand! But how do we come together rather than remain in a downward, divisive struggle for position and power? The answer is simple, yet biblically profound.

God told Abram in Genesis 12 that he needed to do three things in order for him to become a great nation.

Gen 12:1-3 (NIV) The Lord had said to Abram, "Leave your country, your people and your father's household and go to the land I will show you. "I will make you into a great nation and I will bless you; I will make your name great, and you will be a blessing. I will bless those who bless you, and whoever curses you I will curse; and all peoples on earth will be blessed through you."

Americans cannot stay in their old "proverbial" country, people and father's household. They must leave the old and embrace the new.

Each of us must make a decision to first leave our country or ancestry. America is a melting pot of every nation on the earth. Each nation has a history, a way of doing things, and its own set of problems. However, if we are going to become a "great nation" each of us must leave our country and go to a place that God is showing us. If we are successful, God promises to make us into a great nation of blessing. All the people on earth will be blessed through us as we stand as a great nation, united, one nation, indivisible, (not able to be divided) with liberty and justice for all. This is the time for leaders all across the land to stand up and quench the racial tensions. We must begin to say, "We are one! We are a great nation, one great nation, under God, indivisible. No matter what our differences are, we are indivisible. We stand for liberty and justice for all!". I am not hearing these words from any leader in Washington. But I also know that Washington is full of sons of Belial, whose primary purpose in leadership is to divide and conquer. Lately, I have not expected any good thing to come out of Washington, and I have not been disappointed.

Americans of all races and ancestry must leave "their people". This is a huge key to America's future success and unification. As long as the white peeps, the black peeps, the Asian peeps, American Indians, Pakistanis, Philippinos, Latinos and others keep holding on to "their people", we will be a divided mixture or race hating, non communicating groups of segmented color. Divided we fall. But if we could obey God's command to leave "our people", we could meet as a great nation that God is building and we could arise together as one race, indivisible. If a person leaves his people, what color does he become? I don't know for sure – maybe transparent?

I know this fact. I struggled to connect with people of other nationalities and skin color until I publicly made the announcement that I was leaving "my people". I told my church crowd one day in early 2000 that I was leaving "my people" and I was no longer a white man. I didn't know what color I was, but I knew that I was no longer white. Within six weeks, I was working beside some of the best black people that I've ever met, in the inner city of St. Louis, MO. Our church held hands with 13 inner city black churches as we repeatedly delivered truckloads of food to the needy and impoverished. These people are now my brothers and I am connected to them forever. Since then I have worked with some of my closest colleagues and friends in Philippines, Africa and Latin America. I am so glad that I left "my people".

It's time for Americans to leave our people. I recommend that you begin immediately. Go to those you work with, your neighbors, those at your civic organizations, city council meetings, churches and everywhere you can get an open door. Grab the hand of every person who's not your color and tell them with passion and conviction, "I want you to know that I have left my people, in obedience to God's command in Genesis 12. I am no longer a _____ (*your color*) _____ person. I want you to understand that I love you and that I've got your back. If you ever need anything, I want you to contact me and I'll try to help. I am standing with you during times of plenty and times of trouble, and I lay my life down to help you out of any trouble that you ever may come into. I love you and consider it an honor to make this pledge to you."

If Americans would make that pledge to one another in obedience to God, there would be no race wars, no divisions of people groups, and America would rise up into a great nation of blessing.

It's time for Americans to leave our father's household. Every one of us have a story. We all have history and pain. But if we cling to our history and our father's household, we will not become the nation that God wants to make us into. Therefore, we must leave the past, leave our pain, and embrace the new.

We have a Heavenly Father who is attempting to bring Americans into a brand new nation which He will make great. But Americans must leave their country, their people and their father's household, and go to the land that He will show them.

"America as you've known it has ceased to exist" continued . . . This was a hard reality statement for me. My beloved America as I have known it had ceased to exist? What happened? When did she cease? It was a hard reality to swallow, especially because America seems to have a form of life in it today. But I have slipped behind future's curtain and heard the announcement that will soon come to others publicly. So I have been privileged with two realities. The natural reality is setting up to publicly cease in the future, but the spiritual reality has already been shown in the dream, and has given me the warnings of things to come.

Once I got past the harsh realities of this announcement and "realized" *(made real to myself)* that it was a true statement of the future, I was able to move on and prepare for a new America and a new world as I have not known it before. Now I can make some serious plans, change course in various areas of my life, and prepare for a future with a new America and new world.

If you take this dream seriously, you will also mourn the end of your great nation. She ran her race and has finished her course. But now the old is gone, finished and buried *(if the announcement of the dream is true)*. I'm not being "anti-patriotic" at all. I love my country. I am fighting for my country, America's freedoms and the U.S. Constitution. I'll honor and respect my country and those who fought and died to make her free and keep the light of freedom shining brightly throughout the generations. However, as the dream has continually unfolded over the last years, we find that Americans have been displaced and have been left in a land that is not really the nation that they think it is. The three federal branches of government have turned the America that you knew and loved into another nation. Our Constitution is effectively dead. Our Bill Of Rights have been dissolved. Our presidents all work without checks and balances and act as nothing less than dictators or kings, ruling by decree and executive order (which is not constitutional). Non representative Congress is being disbanded and set aside as worthless and useless. The few wrong decisions that they do make are non-constitutional, making them treasonous traitors to "Constitutional America". Many politicians on both sides of the aisle are professionally corrupt and willing to destroy the Constitution, breaking their oaths of office without a second thought or consideration. They swear an oath to defend, and with the next breath they break their oath without hesitation

36

or shame. Corruption and illegal activity are rampant from the top downward. NDAA (National Defense Authorization Act) has destroyed American's right to a fair trial, judge, lawyer or trial of your peers. The court system has been nullified and dismantled because martial law is now in place. The 3/16/12 presidential executive order has given the Feds the right to seize control of your property, cars, bank accounts, businesses, industries, roads, water supplies, food supplies, farms, railroads, waterways and anything else that you own or is considered "yours by law". The executive order allows the feds to force you into a labor work camp to satisfy a need that they may have. It just keeps getting worse by the day and it seems that no one will make a move or stand for righteousness. Those in power seem to know what they're doing, and their covert plans stink to high Heaven among the people who are awake.

Where are the righteous ones in authority? They seem to be nowhere to be found in national or local political leadership. This is truly a day of darkness and corruption as the enemies of freedom are now "within" the borders and have seized the governing powers of our once great country. The fact is that you and I do not have a nation at this time. I'm not sure where you are living, but you are not living in the true United States of America. Your legal documents and rights from that nation are gone. We are immigrants in a new country, one which is soon to be revealed to us, which we will not take "a likin' " to *(as we say in Texas)*. In this new nation, you can lose your right to citizenship because your "right" to natural born citizenship ceased when the constitution died. You are now a citizen by decree of Washington, and when they change their decree you will not have a nation to live in. Where will you go? Some will,

37

actually end up at camp FEMA as people without a country. When the "shockwave announcement" from the dream comes to the public at large, it will be too late to change things, and Americans will be running West for their lives! *(More on where they will be running later)*.

I believe that the supreme foundation of America is, and always has been the Word of God. I believe that it was this divine light and the faith of the fore fathers to find and build a land free from tyranny that inspired and birthed "America". History proves this, although corrupt men are moving ancient boundary stones and attempting to change history by denying Americans a true education about their historical roots.

I also believe that God inspired our founding fathers to create governing documents called the Constitution and Bill of Rights which are the closest earthly example to true freedom in Christ, in honor of God's Kingdom, besides the Holy Bible. These are the best governing documents in the history of the world. They have been responsible for releasing the many blessings of God upon the entire world, starting in the United States of America. This is why the entire world has seemingly wanted to come and live in America! These documents are not perfect. This is why amendments have been made through America's history. However, grave alarm should come to Americans when we see governing forces dismantling and suspending ALL of the Constitution for an unknown, covert and unseen purpose. When Supreme Court justices make comments that indicate the Constitution is outdated and flawed, grave legal trouble is on the way. This is a day for you and I to be wide awake, and responsive to the alarms and warnings that are going off everywhere around us. Wisdom says to take action!

*Prov 27:12 (NIV) The prudent see danger and take refuge,
but the simple keep going and suffer for it.*

America's Constitution and Bill of Rights are not flawed and outdated. If you are willing to look at truth and history, you will see that America was hijacked by foreign entities 100 years ago with the creation of the Federal Reserve world bank cartel that would violate the Constitution and enslave Americans to world banking interests. Congress and then current President Woodrow Wilson were bought and paid for, to sell you and I into the hands of Pharaoh. This was the start of America's downfall. The downward slide has been quickened by the 10 planks of Communism which have been designed and set into place while "we the people" slept. The Constitution could have kept us free and strong, but we left the Constitution 100 years ago and are now going to "Buy the T-Shirt" for the error of our ways.

I am seeing America morph and change as every day passes. The end game of the fundamental transformation is happening very quickly, and some people are waking up to the sound of the alarm. The warning bells of freedom are ringing and the watchmen on the wall are blowing their trumpets to warn the people of impending doom and enemy besiegement. However, many in America continue to sleep. Only some seem to be awake and are rising to see what is really happening around them. Others are awake but are fearful of saying anything because fear of reprisal is gripping them. The dream showed me that the masses, the bulk of Americans in the dream had no idea what kind of announcement was coming to their ears. And that final announcement caused massive, reactionary panic. If you are reading this book today, you are more than likely NOT one of the masses in the dream. God bless you for being awake and prepared during this season.

I am a patriot. However, I will NOT confuse my patriotism for the new socialist/communist country which is being set up on top of, or in place of the true United States of America. I am not patriotic to a new one world order, to a communistic, socialistic, fascist, control grid that dominates people and takes their property, freedoms and futures. My patriotism is for the Constitution, the Bill of Rights, the true United States and the Republic. Anything else and any new fangled ideas that encroach on people's individual freedoms and their right to own property do not have my personal support or patriotism. I hope that you can draw your own lines to where your patriotism begins and ends as well.

Socialism is a philosophy of failure, the creed of ignorance, and the gospel of envy. Its inherent virtue is the equal sharing of misery."

- Winston Churchill

According to the dream, America as I have known her has finished her course. She is now moving into a great testing stage. I believe that she could be moving into a type of cocoon stage. In this cocoon season, she has a potential to transform and emerge as a greater nation than before *(but only if she successfully turns back to the true and living God, trusting and honoring Him and His plan for her miraculous change).* She may emerge into a new America, one greater and better than before. However, if she does not turn fully back to God, America will decline into a third world "has been" which will be known for her past exploits, but who will have no power on the global stage for the world's future. She will join a long list of former super powers who now struggle to reside within their own meager borders, such as France, England, Spain and others who left God and cycled out of history.

In order to embrace the new America which may emerge from the dark time period of the cocoon, we must let go of her past. *(By the way, I don't believe that the new America can prosper without God's divine hand of blessing and protection, and an absolute return to our roots of Christianity and the Constitution. If any of those foundational pillars are permanently removed or destroyed from our nation, America will die in the cocoon.)* Therefore it's important that we all work, pray and resolve not to allow the light of God, Christianity or the Constitution to fade or be ripped out of America's bedrock. The truth and light of the glorious, eternal gospel is the only true hope for America and for any nation on planet earth.

Following National and International Trends: One of my acquired strengths has been to learn cycles, patterns and movements. I'm known by some as the "Giant Tracker TM" because I use the movements of markets, industries, governments and monetary policies to determine the most probable future. When I take the cyclical patterns of the Holy Bible and overlay them with current human events, it's amazing how precise the future can be determined. The process can be explained as simple forecasting using hidden cyclical, historical, and biblical truths. When using historical, repetitive cycles, we can know with high probability what the future is going to look like. Two of the secret cyclical bible truths that I use frequently are:

41

"A Day In Heaven Equals One Thousand Years On Earth"

"First The Natural, Then The Spiritual. First The False, Then The Truth."

Now, let me explain my personal understanding of the times we live in, using cyclical Kingdom secrets from the Bible.

"America as you've known it has ceased to exist." Run from it or embrace it. To embrace will mean that you are ready to move forward with God and His Kingdom plan for your life. You will be prepared to understand your nation as we leave the old cyclical pattern and enter into the new.

Every nation has a cyclical period of birthing, emergence, growth, dominance and then decline. Contrary to our pride and love for our country, America is no different than any other nation or kingdom because she has left God and her roots. America started as a Christian nation, but foreign enemies slipped in among us and took over monetary policy (Federal Reserve 1913). Socialist laws and policies which are contrary to God's economy (Social Security and other acts) include a horrible moral decline which has separated the people from the life, relationship and presence of their God. The rapid cyclical decline from America's pinnacle of success is happening now and is incontestable.

I also believe that we're in the declining cycle of a spiritual day, one of Heaven's days, a period, a season, or an age which is affecting the entire world. Embrace it or fight it, but it's still going to roll in with or without our acceptance. We're leaving a biblical church age (period) and beginning to enter into the kingdom age, period or season. What is this about ages, seasons and periods?

*Hosea 6:1-2 (NIV)1 "Come, let us return to the Lord. He has torn us to pieces but he will heal us; he has injured us but he will bind up our wounds. **After two days he will revive us; on the third day he will restore us, that we may live in his presence.***

The church age (period) has been a 2,000 year period since Christ's death, burial and resurrection. Christ's church has reached out with the message of salvation and revival to the world and all people groups. This time frame is now coming to a close as we're now entering into a third day, a third dimensional Kingdom time frame, according to Heaven's calendar.

Psalms 90:4 (NIV) For a thousand years in your sight are like a day that has just gone by . . . .

2 Peter 3:8 (NIV) But do not forget this one thing, dear friends: With the Lord a day is like a thousand years, and a thousand years are like a day.

The scriptures are clear that a thousand years in the earth are the same as one day in God's Kingdom. Therefore, the 2,000 years since Christ's death, burial and resurrection are the same as two days with God. When you understand Heaven's time frames, we are now entering the third day from Christ *(2,000 years finished)* and the seventh day from Adam *(6,000 years has finished)*. This has profound impacts on times, seasons and changes that come to mankind throughout the entire world. It also has a profound impact on the reason and placement of America in the earth in the mind and purposes of God.

We are entering a day, season, or time period where everything is changing. This will include how America, the church, businesses, governments, nations and people live, communicate, move and look. This new day will determine how your own future will look. The earth is maturing. The church is maturing. America is maturing and changing. Everything is changing. Some things are going to go away, and other things will emerge. Industries will literally disappear and new industries will emerge and take over. This can be a good season for you, your family, your hopes, dreams and visions. You might find that everything you've trained for up to this point is actually for the new season that will emerge in front of us. Where there seems to be no way, God will make a way. A "Red Sea" may open up for you to transport you to a new land, a new field or new dimension of life, work, business, wealth and finance. This could be a time where you emerge into success and everything becomes new around you. But to embrace the new, you will need to let go of the old.

There are people rising up with new maturity, new understanding, new ideas and passions who will be thrust' into positions to possess the kingdoms of earth. They will stand to serve mankind with a new sense of divine humility, power, grace, and direction. They will begin to provide true heavenly answers and guidance to a faltering, desperate world. We have shortages of food, energy, leadership, and financial understanding around the world as fallen man stumbles in his own failures, greed, fear, darkness and disconnect, failing to provide answers for mankind. God has all of these answers and He is raising up a seasoned people who represent His kingdom, who will walk as both "kings and priests" to bring effective change on the earth.

Rev 5:10 (KJV) And hast made us unto our God kings and priests: and we shall reign on the earth.

I believe that we're leaving a 2000 year, second day church age of revival, and we're now entering into the kingdom *(third day)* age of being raised up as kings and priests. As mentioned before . . .

*Hosea 6:2 (NIV) . . . **After two days** he will revive us; **on the third day** he will restore us, that we may live in his presence.*

Believers have known how to serve God as priests in the past. We held wonderful Sunday church services with the best worship, teachings and opportunities to fellowship with other believers. But now we're learning to rule as kings. This will bring a huge change in the world as the priests learn to walk also as kings! The old understanding of Sunday Christianity is about to appear on the 24/7 center stage of business, family, government, education, media and more!

Jesus is the King of kings and the Lord of lords. Whom is the bible talking about when it declares Jesus as King over kings. It's certainly not King Gaddafi of Libya, Egyptian President Mubarak, President Assad in Syria or President Obama in the U.S. "HELLO KING!". "You" are the king that Jesus is King over. You are the lord that Jesus is Lord over. You are being trained in a new day, a new season, and a new dimension of God's Kingdom which is invading the earth. The sun has set on the old church day, and it's going to arise in the new day of kings. You must prepare for this new day that is upon us, and learn all you can about the Kingdom of God and how it functions on the earth.

This raising up of kings will potentially bring America to a great future position of light, liberty, freedom, salvation and authority to the other nations of the world. When I say "America", I say it with fear and trembling, because I now understand that "America" is no longer just a land mass location in the continent of North America, but it's a kingdom reality that's hidden in the hearts of God's people. Many people have muddied the waters of "True America" in their hearts, and they've left the Constitution, Bill of Rights, and the Word of God. They've worshiped false gods and idols of failed socialism, communism, fascism and every other kind of "ism" that's out there in order to try to build a better world apart from God. They're attempting to rebuild the tower of Babylon which is the land of confusion, just like their foolish forefathers did in the book of Genesis before failing in total chaos and confusion *(Gen. 11)*.

The illusion which our lying media, ignorant politicians and even many national leaders give of America is a far cry from God's realistic plan. God's idea of America cannot ever be extinguished from the hearts of people though satanic forces would love nothing more than to extinguish the flame of freedom, liberty, and justice.

According to the dream, there is a strong realistic possibility that Communism could seize the "Terra America" land mass for a period of years or decades, as my dream told me who the number one enemy of America is. However, my first dream did not announce that Communism had won the fight for America. This is what I call a wild card, an unsettled future, and something that can change depending on what decisions the people make for their future. It could go either way, and I am preparing for both, yet praying for freedom and success in "Terra America". While it's possible that the land mass that is currently called the "United States Of America" may or may not rise successful in the future, the "Spirit Of America" will absolutely arise and multiply around the world through the people who carry the spirit of America with them wherever they go.

In Chapter Nine, I will discuss the second dream I had in 2009. It was a dream of utter destruction, but only for a certain group of people. Don't miss this chapter and its interpretation as it will give clues to what happens with the "communism enemy" theme of the first dream.

The Difference Between Terra America & The Spirit Of America.

The fact is that "America" was an idea that was birthed in the mind of God. America has been a successful experiment on earth which has patterned the freedoms and rights of all men created equal, having certain inalienable rights given by God. The Spirit of America is alive and well in the hearts of millions of God's people. But if sin, darkness, and hardening of the hearts of the multitudes continues in the land mass called "Terra America", the Spirit of America may spread her eagle wings and take flight to a different location or locations. She can leave the old "Terra America" for a new, willing, fertile location that will receive the "Spirit of America". I pray that "Terra America" and the "Spirit of America" can come into agreement. But this will depend on the softening and turning back of the hearts of "we the people".

If you are a true blooded, patriotic American who loves God and country, you may be called upon at some point in your future to "take flight" and bring the Spirit of America to a new location on earth where people are hungry for the freedom that you have within your heart. Yes, this would make you a sort of missionary, a bearer of good news, and worker for God's Kingdom. And if the environment becomes too hostile for the "Spirit of America" on "Terra America", the eagle may choose to make her home somewhere less hostile. If the eagle departs, she may never return to "Terra America". This is a horrible thought, but a stark reality that should bring the fear of God into our lives.

Rev 12:13-14 (NIV) When the dragon saw that he had been hurled to the earth, he pursued the woman who had given birth to the male child. The woman was given the two wings of a great eagle, so that she might fly to the place prepared for her in the desert, where she would be taken care of for a time, times and half a time, out of the serpent's reach.

History can point to multiple nations where God's Spirit departed, leaving only a shell of a nation to survive under the darkened, hostile cycles of poverty, corruption and shame. Don't ever be too proud to think that it can't happen in your nation. That same pride has gotten many millions killed by communists in the last 100 years.

Acts 8:1 (NIV) . . . that day a great persecution broke out against the church at Jerusalem, and all except the apostles were scattered throughout Judea and Samaria.

Acts 8:4-6 (NIV) Those who had been scattered preached the word wherever they went. Philip went down to a city in Samaria and proclaimed the Christ there. When the crowds heard Philip and saw the miraculous signs he did, they all paid close attention to what he said.

Persecution scatters the word of God to the nations and actually causes God's Kingdom to grow. Imagine if the Spirit of America were to scatter around the world, like yeast growing in a lump of dough! History shows that God sometimes allows persecution to spread His Kingdom around the world. God's interest is His kingdom. If "Terra America" comes in line with His kingdom, she thrives. If she departs, she goes into outer darkness.

We're entering a Kingdom season - and when kings arise, they go to battle for position, dominion and territory. This answers the question as to why there has been so much international turmoil over these past few years. Nations, kingdoms and powers are fighting for position. We're seeing the kings of the Middle East being uprooted and replaced one after the other. Regimes are ending and new ones are beginning. Governments are seizing control of businesses and industries. Media is making alliances with governments for their own protection. Wars and rumors of war are threatening every kingdom, every nation, and every property line on planet earth.

"First the Natural, Then the Spiritual. First the False, Then the Real."

As the sun has set on the close of an old day, darkness is setting in and mankind is jockeying and clamoring for any position that can be grasped. Satan even knows that his time is short as we come to an end of the second day from Christ, the sixth day from Adam. The season of natural man is going to be very troubled, mixed with un-surety, darkness, discontentment, and destruction as Adam's time frame winds down to a close. But the upcoming season is very "bright" days for the Kingdom of God, along with worldwide implications of biblical proportion.

Mal. 4:5 (NIV) "See, I will send you the prophet Elijah before that great and dreadful day of the Lord comes.

Notice that the DAY OF THE LORD is both great and dreadful? This tells me that it's a dreadful day for Adam, who is passing away and who is losing control of his world around him. His time is short, and the devil's time is short as well. This is why there is such great contention and maneuvering of "kingdom against kingdom" and "nation against nation".

On the other hand the DAY OF THE LORD is also a great day. It's a day where Adam's tyrannical pseudo reign comes to an end and where the Kingdom of God is established forever in the earth, with all nations and kingdoms bowing to His. What a day to be alive! It's both great and dreadful.

Number Seven: Leaving the sixth day from Adam, we enter a brief period of night, and then the seventh day dawns to a full noon day.

Seven is the biblical number for perfection. It represents the day of God's rest as He rested on the seventh day of His creation. It's the last day of the week indicating that the work is finished. It's also the number of Christ, as God's work was completed when Jesus said on the cross, "It is finished!". Jesus Christ is the day of rest, and anyone who enters into Christ's finished work also rests from his own work of trying to be righteous before God on his own.

If man is a three part being just as God works in a three part trinity expression, then it's easy to figure out the identity of the beast 666. It is man's (Adam's) number, 666, spirit, soul and body. Yet there is a perfect man whom we are to relate to, and His name is Jesus, 777. The DAY will reveal this man in you, Christ in you, the hope of glory, spirit, soul and body. This is a profound mystery, but one that will be worked outward shortly in the season that we're entering into.

Number Three: Leaving the second day from Christ's death, burial and resurrection, we enter a brief period of night time darkness, and then the third day dawns. The number three points to the Trinity (Father, Son, Holy Spirit). It speaks of the three parts of man (spirit, soul and body). It speaks of resurrection from the dead and newness of life, as Christ arose on the third day after his crucifixion. It also points to Habakkuk's day three "raising up to live in his site". Day three speaks of the three major Feasts of Israel. The third feast, "Feast Of Tabernacles" has never yet been naturally fulfilled. God uses the number three in many of His expressions. A three cord strand is hard to break.

Eccl 4:12 (NIV) Though one may be overpowered, two can defend themselves. A cord of three strands is not quickly broken.

The tabernacle had three rooms: the outer court, the inner court and the holy of holies. It was the earthly pattern of Heaven. And man is made up of three parts: spirit, soul and body. The number three is one of the most significant numbers in the Bible that speaks of resurrection, salvation, new life and "change".

"First the Natural, Then the Spiritual. First the False, Then the Truth."

Mankind has had 6 days to work this thing out, and has failed miserably. His disconnected, greedy, fraudulent, frail, controlling, lazy lifestyle has brought the world to the brink of mass failure. Now it's time for the Kingdom of God to emerge. "First the natural, then the spiritual." Natural man, then the Spiritual man.

The anti-Christ spirit is attempting to assemble his final "one world order", a full scaled Pharaohistic global dominion of mankind and earth's resources. He will ultimately fail. "First the false, then the truth". The one world order is the false and will be short lived when put up against the eternal order of God's emerging Kingdom rule. God's Kingdom order will prevail and will wipe out man's one world order and its horrible controls and slavery.

Dan 2:44-45 (NIV) "In the time of those kings, the God of heaven will set up a kingdom that will never be destroyed, nor will it be left to another people. It will crush all those kingdoms and bring them to an end, but it will itself endure forever. This is the meaning of the vision of the rock cut out of a mountain, but not by human hands--a rock that broke the iron, the bronze, the clay, the silver and the gold to pieces.

Many believers are trying to figure out the end times, and want to fight over a 3 ½ or 7 year period in the future. They are trying to figure out the micro details of the great transfer from day six to day seven. I encourage you to not enter into arguments which will work themselves out. While quarreling may continue among children, it is not for the mature to argue among ourselves. Understand that the sun is setting on day 6 and will arise soon on day 7. There will be darkness in between which we call night time. But God will give you the tools you need to maintain authority over the night season.

Welcome to the beginning of the true new world order (not the false). God's seventh day Kingdom dimension is emerging with an announcement, and then in full force. This is the seventh day of rest, the end of fallen mans (Adam's) day, the anti-Christ and all that is false and fraudulent.

I am praying for terra America to emerge successful from the cocoon as NEW AMERICA, one with expanded boundaries and borders under the rule of God's Kingdom. She could become great in God's seventh day, if she can be cleansed from the evil rule of Adam's love affair with the harlot and Pharaohistic control over the slave people that he tries to control.

While the "New America" was not in my dream, I believe that this is a real possible outcome for America's future. She must be cleansed, and the cleansing will more than likely come by fire. God promises to bring fire down upon the "sons of Belial". Without going into detail, God has a lot of "sons of Belial" to deal with in America.

If America does not return to her roots and foundations of the Word of God and her Constitution, then her alternate future is one that no decent human being will want to be a part of. She would descend into a dark future of communistic, iron curtain styled, control over the people. The spirit of communism would strip mine the lower and middle class over a period of decades, as this is the true design of communism. The locusts of communism would not stop until everything has been consumed and devoured, and until the will of the people is broken in re-education of submissive obedience to their harsh slave masters. It would be a horrible end as many millions of good people would die, and millions of hopes and dreams would be destroyed in the dark tar pits of despair. Only those who escaped "terra America" with the "Spirit of America" in their hearts would have an opportunity to survive as most of the world would plunge into great outer darkness as a result of America's great fall.

This is a serious time for us all to pray to God for help, salvation and mercy upon our land! If America does not return to God, she will join the other nations of Babylonian confusion.

Rev 18:15-19 (NIV) The merchants who sold these things and gained their wealth from her will stand far off, terrified at her torment. They will weep and mourn and cry out: "'Woe! Woe, O great city, dressed in fine linen, purple and scarlet, and glittering with gold, precious stones and pearls! In one hour such great wealth has been brought to ruin!' "Every sea captain, and all who travel by ship, the sailors, and all who earn their living from the sea, will stand far off. When they see the smoke of her burning, they will exclaim, 'Was there ever a city like this great city?' They will throw dust on their heads, and with weeping and mourning cry out: "'Woe! Woe, O great city, where all who had ships on the sea became rich through her wealth! In one hour she has been brought to ruin!

Chapter 4

Interpretation of the First Dream, Scene 1b –
As I presently understand

----

com·mu·nism:

The advocacy of a classless society in which private ownership has been abolished and the means of production and subsistence belong to the community.

The theory of Communism may be summed up in one sentence: Abolish all private property.

- Karl Marx

"All property lines have been dissolved."

This was the second announcement made by the government official. I believe that this statement has both spiritual and natural consequences in America.

I believe that this government official was announcing to the people that the "RULE OF LAW" brought about by the Constitution and the Bill of Rights in America is dead. The foundation of America is made up of the rule of law, and contract law is a very important bedrock of any society. When a contract is drawn up and executed, it's a document of law which stands all the way through the courts to the highest court in the land. Even the highest court sits under the authority of Heaven to judge "in God's stead" and "under His watchful eyes". So true authority originates with God in Heaven and works its way through judges and to the people through the rock solid rule of law.

When properties, homes, lands, farms, fields, businesses and buildings are built, bought and sold, they are done so under contract law. Every financial transaction in America is supposed to be completed under the contract rule of law. A land survey details the exact property lines which identify the property under contract. Those property lines are as important and set in stone as the contract that they represent - all the way to the Supreme Court of the land who is bound UNDER oath to uphold the highest law of the land, the U.S. Constitution. The Constitution provides the "rule of law" for us to rest, and trust in, to build our lives, families, children businesses, industries, churches and futures upon. Our confidence in the "rule of law" gives us faith and righteousness to invest and build with hope, drive, vision and resolve.

If "All property lines have been dissolved", then something tragic has happened. The rule of law and the Constitution has been dissolved between judges and their commitment "under oath" to God in Heaven. The laws have changed, or those who make and uphold the law have changed the framework that they're going to operate under. This would be an illicit hijack and a hostile take over of God's design for America. Leaders in America must be changing their methods of operation and their fundamentals, and I don't believe this would be done for any other reason than a hostile take over of your life, future and property, destroying your constitutionally framed right to own land and to be left alone to do what you want (the definition of capitalism). In this scenario, you would also become property (a slave) who would be seized upon in order to work for the "collective" purposes of the all powerful, self appointed, god-like government who rules and thinks they own everything (Communism).

There is a property line between my home and my neighbor's home. However, if that property line were to be dissolved, there would be no difference between our two properties, no distinction, no valid contract that dictates the boundaries of our individual properties, and there must now only be one owner. I don't think that this new owner will be I or my neighbor who holds our old property contracts. If the property line is dissolved, neither I nor my neighbor know where the new line really is. Where does my responsibility start and end? Who mows the lawn? Who is responsible if something happens on the land? And is it possible to buy or sell something that has no property line? Am I really the owner, or am I just a slave squatter on a piece of land that was seized from my land through nullification of my contract, dissolution of my property lines, and seizure of my private assets into the collective?

I believe that this statement concludes that our government, in association with other high authorities, are planning a hostile take-over of all properties and people within the United States and abroad. I believe they fully intend and plan to nationalize and own your property and mine by dissolving your contract law and forcefully seizing our assets. They can do this by many different unconstitutional ways including a crashing of the current economy, forcing us into foreclosure and seizure, and rewriting our loan documents to make the federal government the landlord and we the tenants.

There is also a real and living threat of a hostile EPA (Environmental Protection Agency) seizure of your rights as a home or property owner. The green police could license or authorize your home or force you to come into some new strange green law that could effectively cause you to lose control of your home. Imagine a new law or code that forces you to get a home license before you are allowed to sell your home. With that license that is placed on your electrical panel, it will indicate whether your home is "legal" or not. Maybe you need new, more efficient windows, more insulation, a new roof, new siding, or a new air conditioner before you can be "licensed" or allowed to sell your green home. If, and when, this happens (and it's currently in the works) your home ownership is gone and you are only the tenant in Pharaoh's government housing program. You can say you own the home, but you will have no freedom to do what you want with your home. Your former capitalistic freedoms will be socialized, communized and assimilated into ownership of the all powerful federal government collective.

Since the dream took place, let me point out a few ways that the government is actively pursuing the dissolution of your property lines as of the time of this writing.

A. Attack and destroy capitalism. As you may know, there's a huge move to destroy capitalism in America and the socialists/communists want capitalism to disappear. They're pegging the economic troubles and the greed of the bankers and Wall Street to evil capitalism. However, they're spreading deception and a lie. The general understanding of capitalism is: The right to own land and to be left alone so you can do what you want on that land. Since land ownership is the standard of capitalism, then I can presume that capitalism is dead - D.O.A. in America. I do not have the right to own land and do what I want on it, nor have I been free to do so for decades. If I wanted to build a donut shop on my property and fry up some donuts for sale, I would have to jump through zoning, building permits, licenses, plumbing codes, electrical codes, business licensing, signage codes, parking permit codes, food license codes, corporate requirements, sales tax collection permits, employee requirements, a new list of healthcare requirements for all employees, and a list of more codes than you can imagine which are being pumped out of every level of government. No wonder a donut costs two cents to make and $1.00 to buy these days. The customer is paying for all of the codes and statutes surrounding the manufacture of that donut. The government has entered into forced business partnership with every business owner in America. And yet they have no risk. If you start the business, they win because you pay them dearly before you ever open the doors to the business. If you prosper the business, they win big time through taxation. And if you lose the business, they lose nothing. The government has turned into a Pharaohistic, forceful share holder in everything you and I will ever plan to do. I am certainly NOT free to do what I want on my own property. It gets worse.

Try owning a farm and milking your own cow, planting your own food, or trying to sell that milk that you just got from your cow. Can you say JAIL TIME? The fact is that "Capitalism Is Dead", and we must face it. We are not free in this country to pursue the great American dream of property ownership or entrepreneurial investments any longer. There are many other nations in the world which have much greater freedoms and which honor the spirit of capitalism. America has slipped far downward on the totem pole of "business friendly" and free. There are too many hoops to jump through and too many fees, licenses and payments to make to the government for every little thing we would like to do. Welcome to the attempted, fatal, fundamental transformation of America and authoritarian leaders who are not sympathetic to true American values. They believe in big government and government only. They would like the government to seize and own all, to employ all, and to care for all. We call this "COMMUNISM". They call it "Progressivism". Call it what you want, but the sounds of chains dragging at the feet of those who've been caught are not the sounds that I want to hear behind me or my children.

Many of the people who believe in big government have never been successful at maintaining, multiplying and tending their own garden as God commanded in Genesis 1 and 2. Therefore, they slip into positions of power to seize our successful gardens so they can enjoy the fruit of our land at our expense. This will not go well for these "non producing thieves" in the end, and God is taking particular note of their crimes.

B. CAP AND TAX. The government is pushing various forms of "Cap & Tax into law which will be a huge blow against property lines. In effect, it will cause the EPA to come in and have authority to license your home. They will tell you if you're green enough, if you need new windows, more insulation, if you need to change out your roofing, electrical, or whatever they decide they want to do. They will have absolute license to force you to spend your equity in your home to upgrade that home. If you don't comply, you're not licensed. If you're not licensed, you get fined. If you don't pay the fine, you lose your home by government seizure. Pay the piper or get out of HIS home. You also will not be able to sell that property unless your license *(that you will pay a fee for)* is up to date. Can you say, "All property lines have been dissolved."? This will give the government the absolute right to walk across your property line and tell you how to live, what to buy, what to do to your home, and what you cannot do in your home. You will be living someone else's dream - but not your own.

I met a man from the Ukraine who went through the hostilities of Soviet Communism there. He made the horrifying statement, "We pretended to work for them and they pretended to take care of us." Communism will put you in a world of pretend where no one is allowed to dream, to step out in faith, to take risk, or to tend your garden. You will own nothing and therefore will have no personal incentive to take a risk and build. Why build for another man or the government? You will simply pretend to take care of another man's garden, until the horrid system of slavery finally breaks and the people shake free from their chains of tyranny.

C. Fannie Mae & Freddie Mac In Conjunction With Bankers & The Federal Reserve. What a nightmare. There is a covert plan to take over every property in America and own it outright by using your home loan against you. First of all, the totally bankrupt entities called Fannie Mae and Freddie Mac are continually being bailed out by the money printing Federal Reserve – using "we the people's" money that our grandchildren will be forced to pay back in the future. Fannie and Freddy hold the bulk of home loan mortgages right now. If anyone defaults, these government agencies own the property outright. A manufactured famine in the land could cause many millions of foreclosures (like what is currently happening). These foreclosures are a simple transfer of homes and properties into the hands of the Federal Government, bankers, and the Federal Reserve (which is not owned by the government, but is owned by foreign bankers). The story goes deep, but the covert plan is to fraudulently get Americans to enter into a fraudulent document called a home loan. The money is printed out of thin air and you agree to work for 30 years or more and raise the paper currency that they freely create in exchange for your life's work. You pay them back with your life, blood, sweat and tears. And if you default, then the property is fraudulently transferred back into their care, and you lose any investment of time, money and upkeep that you have put in. If enough Americans default on their home loans because home values are falling (under a manufactured money crisis), then Fannie Mae, Freddy Mac and the Federal Government suddenly own all of the foreclosed property in America - for no real money at all, other than the cost to print fiat, fraudulent toilet paper called the U.S. Dollar backed by nothing more than a fabricated promise. This horrible process would end in a tyrannical oppression of absolute police state communism, and the fundamental destruction of your "currently suspended" constitutional right to own land, and to life, liberty and the pursuit of happiness.

What a devilish plan which is playing out before our eyes at this very moment while so many people sleep. It's absolutely astonishing! There may be a few ways to beat the Feds at their diabolical plan. First, pay your mortgage off quickly and do not hold paper with them. Don't put yourself in position to default on your loan payments or your annual taxes and therefore get evicted from "their" rental home. At the end of the day, remember that the loan document and the property tax honestly mean that you don't own your home. If you don't believe me, try not paying either of these and see who holds the title to the property in the next few months or years.

While paying off the loan may help you avert a hostile takeover through loan default or property tax default, it might not shield you from the EPA or other government licensing seizures. The loan document means they really own the property. Also, you may want to sell your home and become a renter for a period of time until all of these acts of war and the re-drawing of property lines are finished. Rest assured, if the Fed takes possession of properties through foreclosure, cap and trade, austerity measures on a bankrupt country, etc., then home prices will fall dramatically. It will be a renter's dream choice market, and you may be able to re-purchase your home for 25 - 50 cents on the borrowed dollar (or whatever currency exists at the time). You might not even want to own a home or land in a communist country, even if the prices seem much cheaper than before, when freedom rang.

In my opinion, there's not much time to get your home sold if you decide to go this route. Prices continue to tumble and the next leg of the United States bankruptcy proceedings will more than likely bring housing down to another new low which could be disastrous to Americans everywhere. Remember that any drop in housing price is by design, to bankrupt the people, and to seize the assets for pennies on the Dollar! Know who your enemy is, and why he is making certain things happen.

Another route to consider is the ultimate; leave the country and go get employment elsewhere. The jobs that have left our country have seemingly landed overseas. I don't believe that they're coming back any time soon, until a total RESET of America takes place and Americans and businesses are once again free to compete in the worldwide market.

Why would a business hire an American for a government forced $15 per hour plus healthcare, social security and other forced taxes? Other nations will allow you to hire their people for $4 per hour with no further requirements. Until America RESETS, jobs will remain overseas and wealth distribution will continue out of America.

You would be celebrated in another country during this time if you looked for employment outside the U.S. borders. What a thought! To think that God could be moving you into a divine mission trip during this financial crisis. I have personally taken action. I've gotten completely out of debt and I sold my home. I've captured my equity before it disappeared through another trumped up crisis, and I'm now a renter until America resets. I am not interested in buying anything unless it's pennies on the dollar for reasons I discuss quite frequently on in my financial education sessions, radio shows, mentoring programs and training. By the way, since selling my home, I can now rent a larger home, nicer, with more square footage - for LESS than it cost me to own my old home. It's a renter's dream world right now in America. I believe the renter's dream world will only get better as housing continues to decline and reset. The supply is high and home owners will bend over backwards to get you in their homes.

Concerning the most important of property lines dissolved, lets discuss the Constitution and the Bill of Rights. These are the most important documents in your world other than the Holy Bible, if you are a U.S. Citizen. They describe the absolute boundaries of the government, the powers, the courts, and the people. If ALL property lines have been dissolved, then the announcement in the dream indicated that the Constitution and the Bill of Rights are no longer acknowledged as valid or legal. I believe that this is exactly what the governing official in the dream was saying. This announcement will be one of the most shocking events for Americans to wake up to, which will cause them to run West in shear panic. Once the Constitution and Bill of Rights are suspended or dissolved, no one in America will have a foundation of any kind to stand on. Americans will be "nationless" in a nation they once knew called "America". Their right to free speech, the right to bear arms, and our other rights will be dissolved and dismissed. When these rights are effectively dissolved in front of "We The People", there will be panic, upheaval and fear like America has never experienced before. This will be the day that Americans head West. (More on heading West in a chapter 8). Once Americans realize that they're living in a land once called "The United States of America", and they see their states dissolved into the collective federal union, they will require retraining into a different America, a different way and a different set of laws and ordinances. I fully expect that this different set of rules will have the stench of the U.N., N.A.T.O. and AGENDA 21. America will be assimilated into a one world, international order who is drawing one new property line around the entire nation, and seizing control of the entire collective that you and I call "The United States of America".

While I hope and pray that I'm wrong on ALL PROPERTY LINES HAVE BEEN DISSOLVED, I believe that what I have stated is true, and that the socialist/communist mindset inside America's borders and government is attempting to nationalize all properties and people, just like Pharaoh did back in the days of Joseph, Egypt and the famine. Pharaoh traded food for land, and when the famine was over, Pharaoh owned all of the land, and the people were just squatters and worked to pay their rent to Pharaoh in the form of high annual taxation. This is the same spirit and historical cycle that's moving in America today. But you can escape the heavy hand of Pharaoh if you act now. Don't expect the bulk of Americans to wake up before it's too late. Make your movements as if none of your leaders are going to rise up and protect America. We certainly cannot trust our elected officials who've committed repeated acts of high treason against the Constitution and our Bill of Rights over the last years.

If you don't expect Washington to produce anything good in the coming years, then you will not be disappointed!

Remember the Bible story of Joseph who interpreted Pharaoh's dream? The story says that Pharaoh had a dream of seven fat cows, and then seven lean cows who ate the fat cows, and who were still skinny and lean. No one could interpret the dream except Joseph, who told Pharaoh that a famine was coming after seven years of plenty, and it would be so bad that the years of famine would eat up all of the seven good years. Pharaoh put Joseph in charge of a plan to save the nation, and they began to tax the people in order to prepare for the famine. Today's financial crisis is like Pharaoh's famine with one exception. This crisis is planned by the hands of men in order to enslave the people and take their property from them. It's a diabolical plan concocted at the World Bank level, and planned a century ago for you to live through at this time. The goal is to fleece the fat greasy and lazy American sheeple and the time for fleecing is at hand.

I think of this Bible story and I have an alternative ending to this horrific story. I assume that the people knew that there were going to be seven years of plenty with taxation. Then a horrid famine in the land would strip all of Egypt bare and give Pharaoh all of the land as the people desperately sold everything for food to feed their families. Maybe they heard it as a rumor, or a conspiracy theory. But no doubt they heard about the coming famine. So if this was the story, why didn't someone crank in the profits for six years of plenty, sell their property on year seven, and then move out of Egypt for seven years? This would have been their salvation, and things would have been desperately cheap at the end of the seven year period. They could come back and visit, or move back and buy anything at pennies on the Dollar. Have you thought about making the same move before the next massive wave of financial crisis hits?

I have a plan that I promote among my clients called "Build an Ark of Safety". I believe that history will prove itself correct again where a few will have an ark of supply and seed. This constructed ark will carry the seed under God's protection during the fire, floods, famine and storms that are going to hit the old economies of the world. Once the ark comes to rest in the new world of the future, the seed will be ready to be released, planted and multiplied for abundance and endless harvests.

68

Check out "Build an Ark of Safety" education that I have available for believers to successfully transport their families, finances, futures and faith into the new world and out of the old. You can find this information at **www.doctordanieldaves.com** .

You cannot legislate the poor into prosperity by legislating the wealth out of prosperity. What one person receives without working for, another person must work for without receiving. You cannot multiply wealth by dividing it.

Chapter 5

Interpretation of the First Dream, Scene 1c – *As I presently understand*

----

com·mu·nism:

A political movement based upon the writings of Karl Marx, the German political philosopher (1818-83), that considers history in terms of class conflict and revolutionary struggle, resulting eventually in the victory of the proletariat and the establishment of a socialist order based on public ownership of the means of production. See also Marxism, Marxism-Leninism, Socialism.

Communism possesses a language which every people can understand - its elements are hunger, envy, and death.

– Heinrich Heine

"The U.S. Dollar is worthless."

When this final announcement was made to the crowd, it seems to have been the catalyst that sent the people into a panic, frenzy and a rush to head West. However, I think that the culmination of the three statements really fueled the last one, causing people to realize that they had been trapped, cornered, robbed and stripped of what they thought they had secured. Their great "American Dream" and everything they knew about their world had just ended with a single announcement.

My study of the U.S. Dollar shows a very gruesome history and 100 year planned seizure of America. From the creation of the Federal Reserve in 1913, private bankers unconstitutionally took over the money creation of our country in a hijacked session of congress that can be defined by reading the book, "Creature From Jekyll Island". When Congress gave up their constitutional authority to coin money for the country, we went under banking slavery through the "DOCTRINE OF DEBT". This doctrine that will enslave and destroy America if she can't come back to her senses and escape from the "pay to play" banker stronghold that is smothering this once great nation.

As the U.S. Dollar has moved forward through time, it has lost 95% of its true value (as of this writing) by design and on purpose. With each step of the Federal Reserve to print more money, the Dollar loses even more value. It is no wonder that the "U.S. Dollar is worthless" because it doesn't have much further to fall before hitting zero $$$ value. The Dollar is the current world reserve currency and it's been historically tied to every barrel of oil produced. This Petro Dollar World Reserve Currency is about to change, and the ramifications are deep, profound, and far reaching for every American and those holding on to U.S. Dollars. The power of the Dollar is going to change quickly and forever in a very near day in our future. When the Dollar loses its world reserve currency status, the world will no longer love, desire or need America! America will hit the skids and everything will change as the Dollar comes to an orchestrated end.

The U.S. Dollar is called "FIAT" currency, meaning that it's only worth what you and other holders think it's worth. It's literally a loan document with a promise to pay the holder the value of that note. That's why it's called a Federal Reserve Note. It used to be backed by gold and silver, but not any longer. President FDR was forced to take the Dollar off of the gold standard for many reasons, and then President Nixon totally decoupled the Dollar from gold in 1971 because the French uncovered U.S. Federal Reserve banking FRAUD. They started cashing in their Dollars for gold from Ft. Knox. They would have emptied Ft. Knox of its gold and there still would have been plenty of printed Dollars all over the world. Why? Because we were printing more Dollars than we had gold to back them up, and we were defrauding the world as men do when they have corruptible powers of the monetary printing press. Our founding fathers knew this would happen if world bankers were given access to the treasury. Therefore, they put protections into the Constitution to protect "we the people". Those protections are gone, unfortunately.

The Dollar is FIAT. It's being sold by the global elite as the best thing that you can own. It's really worthless paper, and costs pennies to create - whether they're printing $1, $5, $10, $20 or $100 bills.

How would you like to have that printing press in your garage? We need a new aircraft carrier and 40 jets to put on it. No problem, let me crank up the printing press. WOW, that's power. How much does a new federal skyscraper cost? It doesn't matter, just print it. How much does it cost to take care of the welfare recipients and to make people happy enough to vote for a certain candidate? It doesn't matter, just print it and let

72

someone else pay for it in the future. How much does it cost to pay the loan back on the U.S. debt? It doesn't matter, just print it. This is our current deception that will destroy America, called the DOCTRINE OF DEBT.

Our money is based on nothing except the promise to pay it back later, with interest - by WE THE PEOPLE, or WE THE PEOPLE'S GREAT GRAND CHILDREN. Now the loan repayment numbers are growing so big on our loans and debt, that they don't even print the money any longer. The Federal Reserve simply adds the money electronically into the banking system with a key stroke, and wha-lah, we can buy just about anything we want, from jets to ships, to military endeavors, to government paychecks, to entitlement programs, to bailouts, to - well - anything we want. The money is created out of thin air, it's backed by nothing, its the LEGALLY DEMANDED currency that all Americans must "by law" use in exchange for goods or services in America and it's highly publicized and sold as high value. But the truth behind the curtain is that the U.S. Dollar is worthless. And the more we spend, bail out and print for our appetites, the more worthless the Dollar becomes. Of the remaining 5% of the Dollar's value that we're holding on to, we have lost 56% of that value in a recent 3 month period. Yet the people don't have a clue as to what's happening. Why? They see the stock market going up in value and they're being deceived by the bankers who are enslaving them. The heat is being turned up on the "almost boiling" frog in the pot, to where the people will soon be boiled completely.

The poorer nations of the world are in revolt because their food prices are sky rocketing. In many third world nations, a family will spend over

73

50% of their income on food to feed their families. So when food prices go up by 30%, they can no longer afford to live. Therefore, they revolt, riot, protest and get very angry! When the world finds out that mass printing of the world reserve currency called the U.S. Dollar is stripping them of their ability to provide food for their families, the world will turn in a fueled anger and hatred towards Americans and you will want to choose carefully where you go on vacation over the next 50 years! They will find out soon enough that AMERICA (actually the world bankers and Federal Reserve puppeteers) has hijacked their dinner table. It will be a dark day for America when they find out the truth. Americans will suffer the kickback, while the world bankers will reap the benefits.

I believe that America will soon face another massive wave of devaluation in the U.S. Dollar. This will be blamed on the European crisis, Iran, Saudi Arabia, oil speculators or the price of rice in China. The blame game will go everywhere except where it belongs, the FEDERAL RESERVE and the world banking elite who own stock in that private corporation. Americans are going to become much poorer in the near future as the Dollar continues to devalue. Some devaluations will probably happen in overnight world trading, and some will come as we see food, oil, energy, clothing and home goods increase dramatically in value. I personally expect that we will see $8 per gallon milk, loaf of bread or a dozen eggs, and $8 - $10 per gallon gasoline as the man made depression sets in and Americans are stripped of their wealth. Grocery stores may be full of goods, but Americans won't be able to buy them. For a period of time, America will become a land of rice and beans in the same way that other third world countries live. The middle class will be wiped out, retirements, pensions, 401k's, IRAs, etc. will be either

74

confiscated or retired as near worthless in the scheme of someone really being able to retire on those funds. The stock market may continue to rise, but it will only be for the purpose to catch up to the failing Dollar. If Apple Inc. stock is worth $500 today, it may need to go up to $1,000 per share just to meet the demands of a 50% devaluated Dollar over the coming season. It's also quite probable that the stock market could take a huge dive when people begin to "HEAD WEST" and look for a safe place to put what's left of their failed currency system.

I have a "Giant Tracker ™" investment target line on my S&P 500 chart which calls for a high probability future price drop to 220 or even 110. If that target would ever be hit, it would mean that Americans have dumped the U.S. Stock Market en masse. Why would they do this? If their country has just been taken over by communism, there would be no further reason to invest in stocks. Communism would now own the nationalized corporate interests and companies that the New York Stock Market represents.

As a side note, how much money would it cost to "buy and own" the entire stock market if you had an unlimited secret printing press?

I fear for the American people because 95% don't know what's happening. It's my understanding that 95% of Americans don't own one ounce of silver or gold! The 5% that do understand what's going on have already taken cover, they've exited the U.S. Dollar and are preparing for life outside of the demise of the U.S. Dollar. They will probably survive this catastrophic wealth transfer nightmare, possibly untouched by the devastation that is to come. However, the herd and the crowd will be financially obliterated, enslaved and fleeced all the way to the skin like a sheep in the sheering stall! And if it's a tyrannical act of communism that seizes control of America, millions of Americans could lose their lives as well.

People in America and around the world are totally dependent on the Dollar. They have their savings in the Dollar, their retirement is in the Dollar, and their mind is in the Dollar. Shoot, everything we've been taught to think is in the Dollar. I will ask you three questions:

1. What is the price of a loaf of bread?
2. What is the price of a normal 3 bedroom home in your community?
3. How much money do you make each month?

The problem with all three of our answers is that you answered in $$$ Dollars! You've been trained to think $$$ Dollars your entire life. Yet these Dollars are the very instruments that have enslaved us, and which will finally steal our wealth, our savings, retirement and future when these Dollars to go ZERO - WORTHLESS pieces of paper that you could use as toilet paper in the end. EVERY Fiat based currency through history has it's end at "$0 - ZERO". None have ever survived. The Dollar is in final throes of convulsion before it dies before our very eyes. Look at the price of gold and you'll see that the Dollar is failing horribly. When the Dollar crashes to zero, there will be such a mass panic that the people will head WEST!

In my dream, the people heard these three announcements and they frantically ran to their vehicles in an attempt to head West. They almost ran over my boy and my friend's son as they sped off in their cars. I had to jerk the boys from the curb to save their lives. I believe that there is going to be a need for some "GOOD MEN" to step up and radically save our next generation from this current generation. Men will need to save them from the frantic decisions that this generation is going to make as they try to save themselves. This generation has learned to throw the next generation under the bus as a daily life style. Good men and women must intervene and save our children and grandchildren.

Prov 13:22 (KJV) A good man leaveth an inheritance to his children's children: and the wealth of the sinner is laid up for the just.

There are not very many "GOOD MEN" in leadership today according to the bible. Those that are in charge are selling out our future inheritance and throwing our children to the fires of the false god Molech in exchange for their own gratification and pleasure today. As a matter of fact, with a true $200 Trillion entitlement debt promised to this generation, our children will be enslaved for 400 years to the world bankers who are running the Federal Reserve and printing the currency to appease our appetite for debt. This is no different than enslaved Israel in Pharaoh's day. The spirit of Pharaoh is alive and well today, sitting in Washington D.C. History's Pharaoh capitalized on the famine in Joseph's day in order to seize control of the entire land of Egypt. Today's Pharaoh is actually creating famines and crisis out of thin air to enslave the people through manufactured crisis.

Debt feels good, until you can't make the payment!

I call this crisis, the "NON CRISIS" or the "CRISIS THAT ISN'T". If you understand fiat currencies and their purposes, you will understand that the crisis is not a true problem, but it's fraudulently induced plan to enslave the entire world to a global elite banking cartel who know the dark magical secret arts of Pharaohistic control.

I believe that God is moving against Pharaoh during this time and he is bringing in deliverers - a type of MOSES that is speaking to Pharaoh to "LET MY PEOPLE GO!". Pharaoh's heart is hard and is entangled in the need for worship from people. God is going to deal with Pharaoh's economy just as He did in times past. God has already started unwinding and unraveling Pharaoh's economy and putting him on notice that he must LET MY PEOPLE GO!. If you believe that this could be the case, then I implore you to read the story of Moses and God's confrontation of Pharaoh (Exodus 4 – 15). You will find a cyclical pattern of how God deals with Pharaoh - and I believe that you will see what is to come in our future as the old biblical cyclical pattern is under way again in America and around the world between the new Pharaoh and God's people.

For all believers who can hear what God is saying, I tell you to GET TO GOSHEN, just as the Israelites did! This is the place where the Israelite slaves lived who were under Pharaoh's harsh control in Egypt. When God began devouring Pharaoh's economy, He totally left Goshen alone. There was a separation of God's people vs. Egypt's people after plague #3. The Hebrew meaning of the name Goshen means: "The place where you go to meet your Father." This is a good time to go meet with your Heavenly Father and get instruction on what to do and where to be. Israel received

78

instruction to bring a sacrificial lamb into their house, cook it and eat it all, not just the parts they liked. They put the lamb's blood on the doorposts of the house. They prepared to leave Egypt by putting their sandals and cloak on, putting their staff in hand, and getting gold and silver from the Egyptians. He told them to get ready to move out and leave Egypt. By this way, they would plunder the Egyptians and would be released from their so called debt burden, re-paid for 400 years of slavery and sent onward towards their own land of promise.

God destroyed Pharaoh's entire economy a piece at a time, and Pharaoh still would not let God's people go. He then destroyed Pharaoh's kingdom future by killing his only son and all the firstborn sons of Egypt. Pharaoh now had no one to leave his kingdom to. He became a one generation kingdom. God ended up destroying Pharaoh's entire army in the Red Sea after Israel crossed over on dry ground.

I believe that at the end of this current historical pattern, the world bank, the Federal Reserve, the global elite secret societies and those who promote war, murder, and division as a business will all be destroyed by God. Their future control over the people will be cut off forever. Deeper study finds these world bankers as "sons of Belial", and they are the personification of the anti-Christ spirit who will be confronted by God and His armies of Heaven, and they will be destroyed by fire or flood. In Pharaoh's case, his armies were destroyed by drowning in the Red Sea.

The story of Pharaoh, Moses, Israel, and Egypt show a cyclical pattern that has revolved over and over through history. It's now happening again. Sparks are going to fly once again as the sons of Belial and the Pharoahistic one world order control grid boys fall into their own traps and hang themselves on their own gallows. However, don't under estimate their illicit powers and willingness to kill innocent people and strip mine nations in order to get what they want.

I believe that part of their destruction will be "wild card events" that happen during their elitist planned destructive efforts. There is no doubt that a small group of world banker elitists have controlled the world, its wars and it's economies for centuries. But their control is going to end as God drags them through Pharaoh's demise. I don't know when or how this is going to happen, but I would guess sooner than later. Earthquakes, floods, tsunami's, solar flares, massive technological setbacks, unannounced weather pattern changes, unintended consequences, earth convulsions, unplanned pandemics that infect even the elite, massive riot outbreaks of people, and shockwave events that come against their plans will disrupt, hinder and eventually overthrow the global elite and their one world order. The BP oil disaster accident in the Gulf of Mexico rocked their world and sent the elite into a short term tail spin, scrambling to recover from their mistake and save face with the world's people. More consequences are coming against their plans of world control and domination. According to the cyclical pattern of how God deals with Pharaoh, the last judgments against them will end their control forever. Be rest assured that God Himself is against them and promises to destroy them with fire.

Since I received this dream, news stories have been posted repeatedly to show the demise of the Dollar and how its losing it's world reserve status and strength. As of now, we know that China, Russia, Japan, India, Iran, and other nations are conspiring to make oil and exchange arrangements outside of the U.S. Dollar. This in itself will be enough to destroy its fiat strength that the people currently believe in. India is buying Iran's oil with gold instead of Dollars. The elite have announced that the Dollar is dead. They began making that public two years after the Lord told me through my dream. The dream has clearly spoken of future events in order to prepare those who hear its clarion call.

As more bailouts come in the future and more Trillions are distributed around the world, this will further weaken the Dollar like water gushing into a glass of Coca Cola. It will be fully diluted soon, and there won't be any confidence in the fraudulent lie called the U.S. Dollar. This is when a sharp decline will come in the Dollar value. The announcement that could drop its value by 40% could happen overnight while Americans sleep and China exits its holdings.

Rejoice if you are one of the few who are living in Goshen. Following God's plan, His principles and His guiding light will bring you into the greatest wealth transfer that the world has ever seen. What once belonged to the followers of Pharaoh and Egypt will soon be yours because of your obedience and actions under God's guidance and light. This wealth transfer will save you, your generation and your future generations, and will put you on your destiny towards the LAND OF PROMISE and INHERITANCE where God wants you to live. This will be a place where you inherit fields you did not plant and live in houses that you did not build. The sky will be the limit: as far as you can see, walk and dream, that land is yours as an inheritance from God. He will take it from

His enemies and give it to His people. This will be a very exciting and powerful season as God's Kingdom emerges. However, it's a very dark and scary time for the people of Egypt and those who live under the fraudulent doctrine of debt.

CRITICAL UPDATE! AGENDA 21 EXPOSED

IMPORTANT UPDATE: Just before going to press with this book, I decided to include information on a horrible plan that is now in public play. I felt compelled to include this information in the section called "ALL PROPERTY LINES HAVE BEEN DISSOLVED!".

In 1992, 172 governments met during a UNCED (Earth Summit) meeting in Rio de Janeiro to discuss global initiatives, which would culminate into a monstrous attack on individual world governments. Today, United Nations Agenda 21 (Google it!) is in full play, and Washington DC is playing with the realistic idea of adoption of Agenda 21. If congress and president sign Agenda 21 into existence, America will be fundamentally changed, the constitution will be toilet paper, and all of your rights will be annulled. This includes the right to free speech, the right to bear arms, and much more. Agenda 21 could literally mean:

1. Private property will be wiped off the face of the earth.
2. You could be forced to live in a single family energy efficient green home at the location of "their" choice.
3. All private farms and farmlands would be confiscated.
4. All private land holdings would be snatched away.
5. All individuals would be banned from owning cars.

U.N. Agenda 21 would also dictate:

1. Where we live.
2. What we eat.
3. How and what we learn.
4. Where and when we can move (if at all).

President Obama has promised to "fundamentally transform America" and is now pushing to implement this freedom-grabbing plan under the radar of "we the people". On June 9, 2011 he signed EXECUTIVE ORDER 13575 and established the White House Rural Council (WHRC). This new administrative body is responsible for federally coordinating and implementing sustainable and green development locally.

An excerpt from EO 13575:

Section 1. Policy- Sixteen percent of the American population lives in rural counties. Strong, sustainable rural communities are essential to winning the future and ensuring American competitiveness in the years ahead.

Watch the word "SUSTAINABLE" which is a buzzword, code word at the UN's 1992 Earth Summit in Brazil (where Agenda 21 was created).

Sustainable simply equals Agenda 21.

UN Agenda 21 is a transnational attempt to erode property rights, destroy freedom and make America submissive to foreign bureaucrats. Agenda 21 is a totalitarian treaty!

Read a segment of Agenda 21 as the UN describes it.

"Effective execution of Agenda 21 will require a profound reorientation of all human society, **unlike anything the world has ever experienced a major shift in the priorities of both governments and individuals** and an unprecedented redeployment of human and financial resources. This shift will demand that a concern for the environmental consequences of every human action be integrated into individual and collective decision-making at every level."

I don't know how else to say it. This is hard core "COMMUNISM" at its core. This UN announcement IS the announcement that "ALL PROPERTY LINES HAVE BEEN DISSOLVED!". In my dream of 2008, when the people heard the culmination of these three announcements, they went berserk and began acting frantically irrational as they headed West as fast as they could get there.

As of this writing, Congress has not passed the bill, and there is a small voice among "we the people" who are faxing and calling to demand that the deaf and blind congress do NOT enact this power grabbing, Constitution destroying UN treaty.

I fear for our nation, our freedoms, and our future. I fear for "we the people" and for the leaders who are blindly headed into great deception. I fear for the lives of leaders who willingly know and have been paid off to vote "yes" on this power grab. I fear because an act of this nature could very well be the beginning trigger of a bloody revolution, a civil war or even a class/race war that could be very deadly and horrific to all sides of the issues at hand. I have committed myself to an agenda of peace, to being a peace maker, and to promoting peaceful opposition to UN Agenda 21. I have also committed myself to prayer for our leaders, for the people, and for the Spirit of peace to hold back anger, hatred and the spirit of murder in the land.

A LARGER, UNSEEN AGENDA:

Many of the things that we see happening around us border on insanity. Politicians aren't listening to the people, they're making decisions that don't make sense to the common American, and lies are being uncovered everywhere. These liars have no fear or shame in lying, and they just smile and cover the lie with another lie. There is no transparency and illegal government atrocities are not dealt with under the full force of law. It's enough to make your head spin. Americans are asking why this is happening, because they can't understand why or how leaders could be so ignorant and treasonous.

There is an unseen, larger agenda that is being pushed which needs clarification and investigation. Once you see the progression of lies and fraud for yourself, then it becomes evident as to why the sons of Belial, secret societies, shadow governments, and others are pushing the agenda. That hidden agenda is "Agenda 21". And the only way Agenda 21 can thrive and prosper is if America is reduced to poverty, with inability to respond to the world's cry for help and rescue when Agenda 21 descends on the masses. This is a very powerful, very evil, and very spiritual movement of one world governance by very sick, twisted, and satanic individuals who sit around and plan the deaths of millions over a cup of cappuccino. They are filled with dark occultic wisdom, having all of the

85

money to buy anyone or any nation they need, and they are absolutely corrupted by their absolute power over the world. They are personifications of the spirit of Pharaoh and they hate the agenda of God to bring life, freedom, and liberty to His people.

It's interesting how Agenda 21 deals with the numbers 777, 7+7+7=21. Remember the rule of "First the false, then the real". Agenda 21 is not the 7+7+7 plan of God. It's a cloaked attempted power grab from fallen Adam, 666. *(see references to man's numbers in chapter 3) This is a hijacking of God's earth and His people, to control, murder and enslave them all under a sick, twisted, multi-headed, beastly authority which receives it's power from the dragon of the book of Revelation.*

I challenge you to go back to 9/11 and re-visit the events of the day in your mind. Study how 3 planes knocked down 4 buildings. Listen to thousands of engineers who have stood up and defied the official story of 9/11. Go back to the Oklahoma City bombing with Timothy McVey and read the sworn testimonies of law enforcement officers who died because they reported seeing Federal agents planting explosives. Review the claim that Osama Bin Laden was killed in 2011, though our own government officials declared on record that he died of kidney failure in 2002. If you can put the story together concerning the "War On Terror", and draw the connecting lines to the current war on terror that's coming to homeland America, then you can see the world banker induced Agenda 21 push which is attempting to disable the only national force of freedom which could stop Agenda 21 in its tracks – the United States of America. Draw the lines for yourself. Come to your own conclusions while the internet is still free to roam. I believe that you will find some of the things that I found as I perused credible documentation from our own government and from credible witnesses who directly contend with the so called, simple "War On Terror" story. It's a frightening thing to consider that diabolical forces are in play right now to bring down the one "super power" nation who can save the world from mass evil.

I thought the war on terror was because of our enemies abroad called "Al Qaeda". How did this war on terror morph to become "Al American"?

Chapter 6

Interpretation of the First Dream, Scene 2 – *As I presently understand*

----

com·mu·nism:

Any leftist political activity or thought, especially when considered to be subversive.

Communism is a hateful thing, and a menace to peace and organized government.

- Grover Cleveland

My Interpretation Of The Dream, Scene 2: As this part of my dream unfolded, I realized that the entire nation seemed to be frantically attempting to go WEST. But some were not trying to go West. Some were already in place and they were the ones who were brokering "consumables" in exchange for hard assets. The man at the gas station wasn't going anywhere, but he was helping others to go West, where they felt that they needed to go. He was going to trade gasoline which the people would need to consume. He would receive hard asset equipment, tractors, mowers, tools and things that would put him in the rental business in the future. So this man, who was Indian (India) in race, would win two times. He amazingly received lots of hard assets in exchange for consumables, and he was immediately thrust into business because of his newfound hard asset wealth. He dictated what he would trade for his gas. He was on the upper end, and people were paying huge penalties to get consumable gas, as they had to give precious hard assets for that gas. And the people were losing a second time. The frantic people were giving up items that had true value, and tomorrow, their gas tanks would be empty. Wealth transfer would have taken a terrible toll on these people.

After much pondering on this part of the dream and many issues surrounding it, I have learned many valuable lessons which I have put into practice in my life for the future. One of the principles that I am now living by and teaching others is: NEVER TRADE YOUR HARD ASSETS FOR CONSUMABLES - NEVER!!!

You see that in this dream; most everyone was unprepared. They were caught in such a pinch that they were frantic, motivated in great fear, and they were willing to trade their true valuables for consumables. People had clearly traded tractors, lawn mowers, large heavy equipment, tools and all kinds of "PAWNABLE" items for a tank of gas. The reality is that these people would burn up that tank of gas that same day, but the man who made the trade would have their valuable asset forever. He would be able to rent it back to the previous owner for even more money, or he could start many businesses with his newly acquired assets. One would lose everything because of being unprepared and in fear, and the other would gain his assets because he was in position, and was patiently waiting for the opportunity to help the fearful get to where they were going. Also, the children of the unprepared would watch their parents trade off their inheritance for something that could be consumed at that moment. This would personify a generation that burned up its inheritance, leaving the children with nothing but debt to start their lives. This is a sin no different than throwing our children to Molech, or to the god of debt. These people were also paying a heavy price to go West. Maybe they could have paid less if they would have gone West a day earlier and could have used the Dollars in their pockets?

Which of these people represents you? This is a hard question to ask, but I've had to ask myself this question. While I know that I must consume food, water, oxygen, energy and land mass (space), I must NEVER be put in the position where I must trade my God given hard assets in order to fulfill those consumable needs. This is a deep subject, and one that I've not seen taught openly in our schools or in business college classes. Only the extremely wealthy understand and operate in this principle.

NEVER TRADE YOUR GOD GIVEN ASSETS FOR CONSUMABLES! Get into position to where your multiple sources of income, your many streams, talents and investments will take care of your needs for consumables and will always overflow to provide investment seed money. Become self sustainable for yourself, and then teach this self sustaining principle to your community around you (if they will listen). This requires DISCIPLINE, PATIENCE, DILIGENCE, SELF DENIAL & PLANNING STRUCTURE. Most people will never choose to walk in this secret until their backs are against the wall and it's too late. I pray that you may enjoy His abundant wisdom in these matters of preparation. For more information on these principles, visit my web site at: www.doctordanieldaves.com .

I believe that there are opportunities for those that God speaks to in reference to this part of the dream. Not only should we be in position to

NOT trade hard assets for consumables, but we can also get into position as the Indian man was. We can help people to get West, and at the same time they will be willing to trade hard assets if we can help them with consumables. Typical consumables that people need during frantic times include: food, water, shelter, security, transportation, jobs, clothing, education and hope. It's highly likely that you could become very wealthy if you position yourself to provide one or more of these products or services to people when they are desperately heading West. *(Heading West is discussed in Chapter 8).*

Chapter 7

Interpretation of the First Dream, Scene 3 – *As I presently understand*

----

com·mu·nism:

Communal living; communalism. The process of communizing or being communized.

I don't really view communism as a bad thing.

- Whoopi Goldberg

My Interpretation Of The Dream, Scene 3: I have always heard that when a president shows up in your dream, that the matter is one of great importance, carrying great weight and authority, and one to be weighed with extreme vigilance. This presidential figure in the dream was President Bush, but more likely that he represents many presidents or "the presidency" throughout America's history, as well as the general authority of America, the authority of the Constitution and the true national authority under which all U.S. law has abided by. It is clear from the dream that the authority (president) has been fighting communism for a long time. With many advisers, counselors, much intelligence and many forms of information, the president, authority, and Constitution of the United States is clearly tired, worn out, and suffering from continued blatant attack against them. The enemy is communism, clear and simple. The authority is clearly tired and worn out as if to throw his hands up in the air in weariness.

I believe that this dream has shown me CLEARLY that the true force behind every evil manifestation during these times has an ultimate end in total dominant control of the people through communism. When I had this dream, communism wasn't on anyone's lips in the media which I was listening to. People were beginning to comment on how socialism was trying to entrench itself into America, but the fact is that America has been a socialist country for decades. I began studying communism, and it would serve you well to study the communist manifesto. Study the 10 planks of Communism (Google it) and learn how communists move in multiple phase strategies to take over a country. We are in the last phase of take over in the U.S.A. as all other covert phases are now complete. Most all of the planks are laid in America without one whimper, one whisper, or one shot fired. The silence of the movement has been deafening! The totalitarian take over is upon us and we are seeing a ramp up of behavior, policies, newly formed laws that destroy what's left of our previous constitutional rights. Police state control is upon us along with an ultimate attempt to lock down the country, the finances, the borders *(to keep us in),* our rights and privileges, and much more.

UPDATE: As of the writing of this book, America is under non stated, soft martial law. The Constitution has been suspended with the overwhelming, treasonous passing of the NDAA (National Defense Authorization Act). This act allows U.S. and foreign military to operate inside the borders of America. It allows military to indefinitely detain U.S. Citizens without formal charges, a lawyer, a judge or a jury of their peers. If the citizen is suspected (a suspect) by the president, his staff or czars alone, he/she can be picked up and indefinitely detained until the "war on terror" is over. The person will forever disappear, just as happened in Communist Russia, Communist China, Communist Cuba, Nazi Germany and anywhere else that communists seize control of. Communism was responsible for the murders of 100 million people in the 20th century. Welcome to the 21st century, and an elitist plan of mass extermination and population CONTROL!

China has announced that they want to have an NDAA law of their own to make dissidents disappear, just like the United States of America has. Since when did the U.S.A. start leading communist countries in ways to make people disappear? We should be very alarmed and making every plan necessary. These are matters of life and death!

What are the reasons for NDAA indefinite detention? This is scary and totally undefined. If a person commits an act that is assumed "BELLIGERANT", that person can be indefinitely detained! The danger is that belligerence can be defined any way needed and changed to fit any political or military desire of the future. I saw 3 acts of belligerence at the shopping mall this week. Does this mean that these people should disappear from society? Is this book an act of belligerence because it exposes the Federal Reserve and the world bankers as "sons of Belial"?

To be fair to the NDAA act, it also gives reference to people who materially or financially support Al Qaeda, or who plan, support, or commit acts of terrorism. This is so open ended and undefined that it could throw America into the throes of a full blown communist cleansing with little effort. This is all constitutionally illegal, yet legal in their new

94

fundamental eyes.

America is under martial law now. How does it feel to be living in the world of fundamental change? The fear and terror you feel when wondering if you could become a target of these vicious martial laws is nothing other than the spirit of terrorism! This terrorism is coming from those who claim to be fighting terrorism. Yet they have just declared the United States of America as a battlefield. And you are the enemy if you are a U.S. Citizen. This is communism at its core. It's nothing less than planning for hard core tyranny, police state, totalitarian control. The foundational laws have been set while the people sleep. However, once the orchestrated depression state collapse ensues, the laws are already in place for martial law and military action. Everyone will be in a wide awake nightmare once it's too late.

The bottom line is this. The Constitution and your Bill of Rights have been suspended by the signing of NDAA. The current illegal legal framework is in place for a Navy Seal team to drop in by military helicopter into your back yard, kick down your door, eliminate any resistance as a military maneuver, zip tie you and all surviving family members, hoist you into that helicopter and whisk you away, never to be seen again. You could be under indefinite detention based on presidential or military belief that you are a belligerent. The Feds will legally NEVER be required to show proof of your guilt, and you will never see a judge. Your extended family, neighbors, your attorney and friends will never be given your location because that will be highly sensitive military information. Say goodbye. You are gone forever! Lights out. Do not pass "Go". Go directly to indefinite detention!

The Expatriation Act is another horrid police state idea which could strip any American from their U.S. citizenship if they are detained under NDAA. What does this mean? It means that they are a person without a country to call home. Where could they possibly go? Well, they're not going to any other nation because that nation would require a valid passport for entry. I believe that they could go to a re-orientation, re-education camp called CAMP FEMA. As of this writing, there are 212+ FEMA camps that are presently manned all around America. Private contractor companies have bid for contracts to man and service these FEMA camps, and the Feds are paying them to be there as of May 2012. And in case you were wondering, the barbed wire is pointing inward, indicating that they are built to keep people IN, not to keep people OUT as in standard security fences.

The Expatriation Act would also issue strong citizenship requirements on Americans including loss of your passport if you ever owe more than $50,000 in taxes. Soon that will change to be $5,000 in taxes. Then it will change to be "Any Taxes Owed". Everyone owes taxes, and the day will come when everyone will be required to stay put in America, barring miraculous intervention from Heaven. The erosion of freedom in America will continue to get worse and worse. There is no need to try to keep this book up to date, because freedoms are being lost daily. I know the following rule to be true:

Expect NOTHING good to come from Washington DC during this period, and you will NOT be disappointed.

The Constitution gives a person who is born inside America the rights of citizenship because it recognizes the authority of natural law which comes from God. These rights cannot be taken away under the Constitution. However, with martial law in place and the Constitution suspended, the Feds can simply decide that you are no longer a citizen and can strip you of any right of travel, to live and work in America or anywhere else in the world. The very root of this illicit authority is unconstitutional and tyrannical. However, it's right in line with communism.

In my opinion, America has been hijacked from communist forces from within who are allying with communist forces on the outside. Many others have been paid off and bought in order to go along with the covert plan which my dream from God revealed. How much does it cost to pay off hundreds of people in Congress, some legal departments and some federal judges? Well, how about the uncovered $16 Trillion that the Federal Reserve secretly printed and handed out to their friends all over the world during the first bail out while we thought we were arguing over $787 Billion? That amount ought to be enough to cover the pay off. That would be $1 Million each for 16 million people, or $8 million each for 2 million people. What about the Trillions $$$ more that have been covertly printed and distributed which we have not yet made public? How much does it cost to buy off Washington DC? How much to pay off major news outlets? Who cares, just start printing it and handing it out. That's what we do in America since adopting the DOCTRINE OF DEBT.

You can only guess what's going on behind a non transparent, fraudulent, lying institution that swore an oath to uphold your constitutional rights. Oaths and talk are cheap during this season! And when elected officials swear and oath and break it, they will pay the consequences directly to God whom they swore the oath to.

This is a very dangerous season for Americans, yet so many are asleep or totally unaware of the trap that's been laid. I pray that you are fully awake and that you can get into Psalm 91 protection from almighty God before the curtain, the hammer, and the sickle drop down around you.

Remember that when I had this dream, I heard almost no one talking about communism, totalitarian control, the police state or martial law. Although, there were some who were wide awake well before my dream. Today, communism is a buzz word and the communist enemies are moving out in the open rather than covertly. They're out in the open and they're coming for our fleece, property, wealth, our children and our slavery.

There are only a couple of things left that I can personally see which stand in the way of a totalitarian take over of America by hard lined communists. And by the way, I don't believe that Obama is necessarily the hard·lined dictator. I believe that he is the soft tyranny dictator who will make way for the hard lined hammer. As Lenin made the way for the horrible Stalin, so Obama is making the way for the horrible _____ (fill in the blank). This guy, whoever he is, must never be given the platform of president/king/dictator over what's left of America or it's going to be very bad for the people of the U.S.S.A.

Some states might threaten to defect from the union if martial law is ramped up and activated with federal or foreign troops in the streets. This defection will more than likely be met with Federal military and political action against those states. It might look like the weekend warrior National Guard and the local Sheriff's office standing up against Army, Navy, Air Force, and Marines. Remember the Civil War and when the North fired on their own Southern citizens? Don't expect anything different to come out of Washington as evil forces seize and maintain power and control.

The other stronghold that Americans hold against communism is millions of guns held by millions of "We The People" citizens. However, getting these millions of people together to risk their lives, indefinite detention, or loss of citizenship would be a very hard thing to do in this day and age because "we the people" believe that we still have too much to lose. The patriots of 1776 had lost everything. They had nothing left to lose. They said, "Give me liberty or give me death". Americans today say, "Give me liberty, or at least give me something…. Maybe a bail out?.......Please?" Americans will be fearful of loss as long as they still have digital zeroes in their supposed bank accounts and as long as they still believe that they own their homes, cars, and trinkets in the closet.

"Hope. It is the only thing stronger than fear. A little hope is effective, a lot of hope is dangerous."

- President Snow in "Hunger Games" movie.

I fully expect a government orchestrated, heightened opportunity for Americans to be forced to make a decision of "fight or flight". They must turn in their guns under martial law, federal mandate, for the supposed safety of the nation, under U.N. treaty or something contrived as a good thing. Maybe a race war will require federal intervention, martial law and a presidential order to turn in all guns. If people refuse to turn in their firearms, they will be guilty of a felony crime, or will be threatened with loss of citizenship, guilty of NDAA rulings, and they will be considered belligerent, terroristic, to be rounded up, re-educated, killed or simply made to disappear. Once you see the push for gun control take effect, you will know that the last cards are being played. A fearful, submissive, disarmed America will be an easy target for communist domination. Disarmed citizens are no more than slaves under the control of those who are armed.

Police departments and military are being trained right now to use overwhelming, lethal force at the sign of any resistance whatsoever, as the time comes to confiscate weapons from door to door. Overwhelming lethal force doesn't sound to me like America as I have known it.

A civil war or overthrow rebellion would be a very bloody one indeed. Many people would die during this move as resistance, rebellion, freedom fighters, and Billy Bob in general could potentially come out of the woods shooting. They would be dealt with by government, federal forces, foreign and federal military, and would probably be considered terrorists, just as George Washington and the 1776 patriots were labeled. When you see American troops shooting Americans or foreign troops on U.S. soil shooting at Americans, you must know at that time that the dream was true and correct. I personally pray that there is NEVER a shot fired, because this would be the shot heard around the world which would bring the end to America as we have known it, and the end to so many precious American lives. War is hell, and I pray that hell will not come to America!

God, I'm begging you for divine intervention as an act of mercy.

Will God help America? I wish I could be confident that He will. However, Americans have been so hard hearted, so rebellious, and so anti-Christ in our nature, that we literally have become enemies of God through our beliefs and actions. America has removed God from every form of education, government, the courts, and society. America has turned to horrible demoralization and sinful alternative lifestyles that are biblically judged as worthy of death. Americans have thrown 53 million plus unwanted babies at the feet of Jesus, and now we're discussing whether or not we can kill them while they're infants, with no intrinsic value until after they are two years old. We're also death paneling senior citizens and in a hardened way we are plotting the deaths of anyone who is "undesirable" or who is not a strong producer. I believe that certain judgments are coming up on a rebellious and obstinate people who MUST turn back to God before He will withhold His hand of judgment. We commit a 9-11 every day, killing more than 3,000 children per day in our nation, and Americans wake up, go to work, play, eat, drink and party without even thinking about those innocent murdered children whose deaths are sanctioned by our own legal system. And we want God to step in and help our job situations and freedoms? What about the rights and freedoms of those children who were murdered? Give me a break! A man reaps what he sows. It's time for Americans to turn back to God or suffer judgment and correction by the northern armies that we'll call

"Communists".

Could it be true that God will require one American life for every life that we have murdered in the womb? That would be 53 million American lives lost under God's hand of judgment. Interestingly, communist strategies believe that between 50 – 60 million Americans will need to die in order to subdue America and fully communize her.

Please remember that we are living under "quietly induced" martial law. This means that time is short before the sparks fly and martial law is enforced. At that time, it will probably be too late to take evasive action to save yourself and family. The time to prepare was yesterday. Time is short and if you're just getting started, you are way behind the curve.

If you take an extended international vacation, you will probably need to take extra clothing and supplies. Communists don't leave quickly and this attack on America won't be a McDonalds drive through moment. Communism is used by the banking elite cartel to strip mine a nation all the way to its core. America has been fat and wealthy, and she has tons of oil and natural gas reserves underground. A prolonged term of hard line communism would strip the wealth, independence, liberty and sovereign pride right off of Americans. Those that survive the onslaught would have been re-educated and humbled, impoverished, and enslaved. I pray that Americans will not allow this to go the way that the communists have planned. A return to God is the first step to salvation from onslaught.

None of us like to think about America becoming a hard lined, oppressive, communist, police state. However, the potential is absolutely upon us, and a person would be a fool to not plan for this possibility. If America falls to communism, it will not be a 12 month stint and then "we the people" will vote them out and bring change. Rather, communism normally plays out over a 40 year period or longer. These guys don't leave quickly, easily, and without a fight.

Communist Russia started under Lenin in 1917 and ended in 1991, 74 years.
Communist East Germany 1949 - 1989, 40 years.
Communist Mainland China 1949 - Present, 63 years and counting.
Communist Czechoslovakia 1948 - 1989, 41 years.
Communist North Korea 1948 - Present, 64 years and counting.
Communist Cuba under Castro in 1959 - Present

Therefore, if you plan to stay if America falls into the hands of hard liners, then you must plan to stay through the duration. Your food, energy, bullets, and clothing will not last 40 plus years of harsh tyranny. Remember that you will need re-training and re-education, simply because you read books like these. If you can't be retrained, you must go away and disappear. You and your family will be subjected to lines, lack, tyranny and things that you would never want your children to see or experience. People will disappear and not return. Your countrymen will either sell out to the system for their own survival, or they will fight and disappear. Everything will fundamentally change until America is strip mined of every spare dime, every natural resource and every ounce of fat and financial wool from the sheeple. Those who disappear will be the hard working, principle driven, well educated, morally strong people of your community who brought strength and support. The single word to sum up the experience will be "brutal".

"The land of the free and the home of the brave" will effectively be removed from the memory and psyche of the American citizen, so that only submission, fear and slavery remain. Americans will learn to walk quietly with their heads down, not making eye contact, or drawing attention to themselves. Visit a former communist nation and see the hardness, bitterness, fear and submission on the faces of the people. This is the only way to survive behind an iron curtain of surveillance, absolute authoritarian rule, tyranny and commanded absolute obedience. Again, it will be "brutal" for all who survive, if you want to call it survival.

Would God allow such a thing to happen to America? I'm not sure He will intervene to stop it. What should the righteous national punishment be towards a people who collectively kicked God out of His own nation, who elect politicians with fruitless, treasonous views and lives, who've murdered 53 million plus innocent babies, who repeatedly break the law and start unconstitutional wars for profit, giving full access to non patriotic world bankers to strip mine the blessings that God gave to America, and whose people refuse to return to God in repentance? What about our worldwide promotion of godless immorality? Are we representing God and His interests in America? Are we "One Nation, Under God, Indivisible"?

I personally am not interested in aligning myself with a rogue nation who hates God in deed and action. I have decided to align myself with the

Kingdom of God and His righteousness rather than to suffer with the disobedient. That's my personal decision, but I don't criticize your decision. Just get to where God wants you quickly. Now is the time to draw your own hard boundary lines before your enemy tries to dissolve them.

The only good news that I can see behind this "communism" part of the dream is that while communism is in its last and final take over phase, the dream did not say that America fell to communism. While the dream in scene one showed a mass panic because of the announcement, nowhere in the dream did America actually fall to communism. I believe that many communists or sympathizers *(many of them deceived or offered power which corrupts)* are in control of a large part of America at this time. I also believe that the communist plan is making a final attempt to control all of America's three federal power branches of government and the military.

There is a second powerful presidential dream that I had in 2009 which further clarifies the future for America. This dream and its interpretation will be explained in chapter nine.

Isaiah 40:31 (KJV) But they that wait upon the Lord shall renew their strength; they shall mount up with wings as eagles; they shall run, and not be weary; and they shall walk, and not faint.

My prayer is that THE MIGHTY EAGLE will raise up with renewed strength and with God's hand of help, it shall bring in God's Kingdom of freedom, liberty, justice and constitutional revival. This would unveil and reveal the enemies of freedom, and cause the people of America to unite and bring about a clearly defined constitutional revival through peaceful revolution. That is my prayer and my hope. However, I still see many of "we the people" walking in great darkness, deception and gullibility, following any and every trend, swaying back and forth between kingdoms, voting their pocketbook, their party or race, rather than standing on morals, principles, godly conviction and laws of Heaven. So I also pray for their blinders to be removed, and true godly repentance to be GIVEN (which God is not required to do). I pray for a revival, renewal and restoration of God's divine life and goodness through Jesus Christ to all men, so that they can see the enemy that is attempting to chain and captivate them with the plans to destroy them and their children's future.

(Isa 60:1-5 NIV) "Arise, shine, for your light has come, and the glory of the LORD rises upon you. See, darkness covers the earth and thick darkness is over the peoples, but the LORD rises upon you and his glory appears over you. Nations will come to your light, and kings to the brightness of your dawn. "Lift up your eyes and look about you: All assemble and come to you; your sons come from afar, and your daughters are carried on the arm. Then you will look and be radiant, your heart will throb and swell with joy; the wealth on the seas will be brought to you, to you the riches of the nations will come.

Chapter 8

My Interpretation of "People Heading West"

----

com·mu·nism:

A system of social organization in which all economic and social activity is controlled by a totalitarian state dominated by a single and self perpetuating political party.

I have taken an oath in my heart to oppose communism until the day I die.

- *Eldridge Cleaver*

In the first section of my 2008 dream, the people heard three announcements which caused them to frantically head West. I believe that this requires interpretation, as I just can't see the nation running to California, Nevada, and Arizona for protection from the three announcements.

As an educator of biblical theology, I have a particular thought of people heading West which I have gained from my studies of the Bible. I want to express this thought because it brings hope into the dream that I had.

Historically in America we know that West was the direction that the trail blazers, Lewis & Clark went, as well as, the wagon train settlers and those who were staking a claim in America. From New York, Boston and other East coast cities, the people began to move and settle out West. Therefore, West is the historical movement of Americans when they are moving in progression. Is it possible that the three announcements are forcing Americans on a progressive path to a new America and possibly a new world order?

Biblically, West is indicative of the setting sun and night time. It's the middle of the day in God's Genesis viewpoint. Everything He spoke in the first six days of creation began in the evening and ended in the morning.

Gen 1:5 (KJV) And God called the light Day, and the darkness he called Night. **And the evening and the morning were the first day.**

According to the Genesis pattern, when God speaks a creative word into the earth, He does it in the evening as the sun is setting. Then the night time comes to test the word as the sun sets in the West. When morning dawns and the sun rises to the full day sun, His work will have been proven through the beginning night hours. Interestingly, the Jewish day starts at sundown in the evening. This is why the legs of the thieves were broken on the cross beside Jesus so they would die before the Sabbath, which started at sundown that evening.

West translates into the setting sun. People in my dream were running West in a panic. I believe that they were symbolically running towards a new day and the birthing of the biblical "day number seven" which I discussed earlier in this book.

In the Old Testament pattern called the Tabernacle of Moses, this tabernacle was built on earth as a direct representation of the tabernacle in Heaven which Moses saw. This Tabernacle has many hidden keys to life for mankind and it's well worth studying.

The entrance to the Tabernacle is in the East, called the Eastern Gate. This Eastern Gate is symbolic of Jesus Christ, who "IS" the gate, the door, and the way.

John 10:9 (NIV) I am the gate; whoever enters through me will be saved. He will come in and go out, and find pasture.

John 14:6 (NIV) Jesus answered, "I am the way and the truth and the life. No one comes to the Father except through me."

From the Eastern Gate there is a progressive movement towards the West, from the Tabernacle's outer court, to the inner holy place and then to the holy of holies. The priests would make their progression Westward every day in their service to God, and the high priest would head West all the way into the Holy of Holies once per year to offer a sacrifice of blood to God for the sins of the people.

With this understanding of the Tabernacle and Westward movements towards God, I gain great hope that Americans will be frantically heading West, towards God and towards their roots, heritage and national foundation which our fore fathers established America upon. It's very possible that the dissolution of the Dollar, property lines, and the nation as we have known it will bring the people to their proverbial knees, and a great return to Christ will happen across America. However, the dream makes it clear that the return will not happen until it's too late to save property lines, the Dollar, or America as we have known it.

I don't believe that America can be restored until Americans return to God, their roots, and America's foundations. If the frantic Westward movement of Americans in the dream signifies that they are returning to their roots and their God, then this brings me great hope.

We are entering into a new day. It's starting at sun down, the same way that God did it in Genesis. This new day will be one of a beginning restoration. Will it signify a New America? Whether or not America survives, I believe that God is starting day number seven. It's a day of God's Kingdom, and it will culminate in a great victory for all who love God, who love life, and who consider God's way as the only way for them. This will not be a good day for evil, for wicked people, or for anti-Christ, hate filled, controlling elitists who hate God and His plans for abundance of life.

I pray that America takes part in "Day Seven". I've heard many scholars say that they can't find America in their versions of apocalyptic prophecy. Maybe a new America is arising which has not been previously considered. Regardless, we know that the kingdom of God is at the door and time itself is pressing the entire world into Day Seven.

When Americans frantically return Westward, they will do it without their old America, without property lines, and without a U.S. Dollar. Indeed many things will end and many new things will begin at that time.

Chapter 9
My Second Dream and Its Interpretation, August 2009

Marxism:

The doctrines developed from the political, economic, and social theories of Karl Marx, Friedrich Engels, and their followers: dialectical materialism, a labor-based theory of wealth, an economic class struggle leading to revolution, the dictatorship of the proletariat, and the eventual development of a classless society.

I know that I am leaving the winning side for the losing side, but it is better to die on the losing side than to live under Communism.

- Whittaker Chambers

In August of 2009, I had a similar dream to the first, where I was deep sea diving with a group of men, and President Barak Obama was the lead diver. *(I was there in the same powerful, realistic way as in my first dream).* We were down deep in the ocean and had full face masks with intercoms so we could communicate with each other. I am an open water diver, and I remember feeling that we were deep enough that we would need times of decompression at higher levels if we headed back up to the surface. I could hear President Obama speaking and giving directions. We had swum into a wide entrance of a deep cave and there were multiple tunnels on the other side of the large structure. I remember having the feeling that we were in great danger because we were down deep, and we had a lot of rock up over our heads. *(As an "open water" diver, I don't like having structures over me that would stop me from surfacing in an emergency.)*

As we shined our diving lights towards the tunnels on the other side of the cave, I noticed one tunnel that was very murky. The silt and sediment filling that tunnel was so thick that we could never enter that outlet without only feeling our way around in there. It seemed very dangerous as we would clearly lose our way if we went into that outlet. The other outlets didn't look murky, but they were very dark.

I remember feeling very uneasy and an alarm was going off inside of me. I knew that I needed to get away from this group, and I needed to get out from under this cave and into open water. While I was considering whether to leave the group, President Obama said, "We can't go into that murky tunnel over there." Then suddenly an earthquake shook us and a huge pile of rocks fell down and closed off our entrance to the cave. We were trapped inside the cave, and I quickly realized that we were going to die. We had limited oxygen and there was no way to move the many heavy rocks blockading the mouth of the cave. Moving along inside of that cave with President Obama and the others that were along with him, led me to being at the wrong place at the wrong time. I was on the wrong side of a very bad earthquake and death was inevitable to everyone who was on that dive team. I remember feeling sheer terror and fear, knowing that I was going to die by drowning. I then awoke from the dream.

MY INTERPRETATION OF THE DREAM:

I believe that this dream took place deep under water as this is the current

112

condition of the U.S. and world economies, as well as our political, spiritual and mental condition. Every national economy, every fiat currency, and every governing politician is "deep" in moral, spiritual, political, and financial debt and deeply under water in their ability to lead. Instead of attempting to head to the surface, the president and his team were swimming sideways heading into a cave, looking for a good tunnel to swim into. I believe that this signifies a government leadership who is content to continue in debt rather than coming out from the national debt that is mounting up quickly in America. It also signifies to me that Washington, D.C. is moving in a covert, unannounced, one world agenda that is taking the nation sideways and towards deep, dark, murky tunnels, instead of up and out of danger. Because this group is willing to dive deep and enter into dangerous territory, they will purposely and by design, be trapped when the financial, moral, spiritual, and ethical earthquakes hit.

Whenever a president enters into a dream, I understand that this is a very important dream. And I also believe that a president is symbolic of "we the people" and the represented leaders of that nation. The fact that my first dream had President Bush and this second dream included President Obama is not necessarily an interpretation of the actual presidential men. I believe that the president in this dream signifies the Federal government in general. "We the people" are content to allow our politicians to lead our nation deep into debt. We are willing to endanger our national security by going deeper into debt. We are willing to go into dangerous caves where there is no clear path back up to the surface of zero debt.

When becoming licensed to dive, the first ranking is "Open Water Diver". This means that the diver is limited to a certain criteria including

"Open Water" over your head at all times. If there is ever trouble, there must be an open opportunity for you to get back to the surface. If a diver wants to go into caves where there is no clear path to the surface, more extensive training is required. The risks of death are multiplied when you go into a cave, into a sunken ship, or when you put a roof over your head and limit your ability to surface and find air.

Understanding these dangers in diving helps me to know why the presidential dive team is in such danger. They were considering going into deep, dark, murky caves while on their exploration. The cave we were in was already dangerous. But entering the dark tunnels would be even more dangerous, murky, and easy for divers to lose their judgment, sense of direction, and equilibrium.

An earthquake hit at the wrong time while the dive team was in the wrong place. The shaking was so strong that huge boulders fell over the mouth of the cave. These were the 1,000 pound type of boulders that would clearly not be moved by any team of fin flapping divers. We were trapped, and we were not going to get out alive. We would die from oxygen starvation and drowning (in debt), being trapped in a cave that we knew was very dangerous, but which we had decided to be in anyway.

I believe that this is very symbolic of anyone who is following the lead of Washington, D.C., and the general so called two party election process in America. I believe that a proverbial earthquake is coming to America that will trap anyone who's on "Dive Debt Team America", and there will be no way out for the nation or individuals who are in debt. How could this happen?

According to the mathematics that I subscribe to, America crossed the

114

point of no return into bankruptcy and financial default at $12.2 Trillion Dollars of debt. Washington, D.C. crossed that line without a single debate, and without a single worry that America needed to pay off debt and come back from dangerous bankruptcy. Since then, we have racked up Trillions more in debt, and America has spent more indebted Dollars in the last few years than America spent in the last 100 years altogether. We are spending money that we don't have like drunken sailors on a 24 hour leave! There is no care or concern about the debt, and Americans on both sides of the isle are treating this debt as if it were normal. Even "we the people" are in more credit card, home loan, college tuition, and unsecured debt than we have ever been in history. Doctrines flow from the top down, and "we the people" are addicted to debt!

After the $700 billion bailout, the trillion-dollar stimulus, and the massive budget bill with over 9,000 earmarks, many of you implored Washington to please stop spending money we don't have. But, instead of cutting, we saw an unprecedented explosion of government spending and debt, unlike anything we have seen in the history of our country.

- Michele Bachmann

News commentators talk about the national debt with little concern, and it seems as if it's almost fun to talk about. Meanwhile, every new Trillion $$$ we spend is putting another generation of children into slavery and debt. We are throwing our children and grand children's futures into the fires of Molech as we sacrifice them for the sake of our own brief pleasures and benefits. As it stands, someone is going to be required to pay the national debt off to the World Bank who is printing and loaning the money to us under the cover of the Federal Reserve. Our children and great grandchildren will end up hating this present generation for the gross abuse of power and the absolute mishandling of the power of money as they live in third world debt, poverty status, owing a debt that they cannot pay.

"The doctrine of debt is what will destroy America."

- Dr. Dale Sides

"If the American people ever allow private banks to control the issue of their currency, first by inflation, then by deflation, the banks and corporations that will grow up around them will deprive the people of all property until their children wake up homeless on the continent their Fathers conquered...1 believe that banking institutions are more dangerous to our liberties than standing armies... The issuing power should be taken from the banks and restored to the people, to whom it properly belongs."

- Thomas Jefferson

Prov 13:22 (NIV) A good man leaves an inheritance for his children's children, but a sinner's wealth is stored up for the righteous.

America has sinned greatly by giving away our constitutionally held right for Congress to coin money to the World Bank, aka Federal Reserve. We sinned when we took the Dollar off of the gold standard and entered into full fiat currency. We have greatly sinned when we stepped over the point of no fiscal return, securing our future in bankruptcy and default, without even a hesitation. Therefore, America deserves to go bankrupt. America deserves to lose her world reserve currency status. America deserves to fall into third world nation status because we have sinned against the laws of finance, the laws of mathematics and the laws of God.

Deserve (verb) - *be worthy or deserving; to have it coming – deserve, either good or bad; www.thefreedictionary.com*

We have embraced debt and forsaken the commandments of God to stay out of debt. We deserve what is coming. The earthquake that will sink America is the one that we have created. We've enjoyed the credit card, and it's about time to pay the piper. Since we can't pay, we will be forced to pay in bankruptcy proceedings. I believe that this is the meaning of the great earthquake which trapped "Dive Team America" in a deep cave with no escape possible.

How could we be forced to pay America's $16 Trillion, $20 Trillion, $25 Trillion debt, along with the $200+ Trillion in unfunded promises that Washington has assured "we the people" that will be coming to us in the future? Let's take a look at a few potential scenarios, but these are clearly not an exhaustive list of possibilities.

The first scenario is a devaluation of the U.S. Dollar currency, which has already happened and is continuing its decline on the way to $0 value. Every time the Dollar devalues, it allows the government to pay off its horrendous debt with cheaper money. Unfortunately, this means that "we the people" will pay the price by losing our savings, retirements, and anything denominated in worthless toilet paper Dollars.

Scenario #2: I believe that the government is already making payments to the elite of the world whom we owe. America owes China Trillions $$$ and China is now being allowed to buy up banks, media companies, and other industries in America. In other words, China is staking a claim over the brick and mortar institutions inside of America, and is buying these businesses with worthless, fiat Dollars that they hold. Washington is also cutting deals with elite oil institutions, and will end up giving away the Trillions $$$ in oil reserves that America holds underground in Alaska, the Dakotas, Colorado and elsewhere. Washington is also giving direct access to the U.N. and the horrid "Agenda 21" plan. The new international sea treaties, gun treaties, farm and habitation treaties are signing away national sovereignty, privately owned farms and lands, and making America a free for all for seizure for any international elite that we owe. Washington is also planning for the default of the U.S. Dollar and the resulting mass chaos, rioting, and civil war that will follow in America. NDAA and presidential martial law and seizure executive orders are in place to control the masses, seize property, industries, transportation, and more once they pull the plug on the Constitution and attack America's sovereignty. Lastly, Washington is planning to use a huge financial collapse to allow confiscation of home and commercial property as they default under debt obligation to the World Bank, aka

Federal Reserve, Fannie Mae, and Freddy Mac. Americans are going to find themselves homeless and only slave renters on the continent that their forefathers previously conquered. This is nothing different than a biblical re-make of Pharaoh's created famine in Joseph's day. Pharaoh seized the lands and farms of the people in exchange for taking care of the people during the famine of Genesis 41.

Unfortunately, "We The People" will be the last ones to find out about Washington's and the world elitists plans. When the earthquake hits, "we the people" are trapped, and when "we the people" finally hear and understand the three statements from the government official *(in my first dream)*, they're going to be ticked! There's going to be such a house cleaning spirit in America that Washington is fully prepared to defend themselves with military action, UN troops on America's streets, martial law, and indefinite detention of the angry mobs which they will call terrorists. It's going to get ugly. A lot of people are going to die, and Washington is preparing to defend themselves after their own house of cards falls around "we the people". Unfortunately, "we the people" will be the ones who pay dearly for Washington's massive errors and failed policies. Our doctrines of debt and our willingness to allow them to take us into the deep, dangerous cave of darkness will bring us the results that we deserve.

America is going to be reminded that there's only one who forgives sin and pardons debts. That one is He whom we have forsaken.

Psalms 79:9 (NIV) Help us, O God our Savior, for the glory of your name; deliver us and forgive our sins for your name's sake.

The continuation of this earthquake collapse will include an absolute end to government services and promises that the federal, state, county, and city governments have promised to "we the people". I believe that Social Security will come to a halt. Healthcare will go to third world status. Food stamps, welfare, unemployment, tax breaks, HUD and housing subsidies are all going to go away. When the people need food, Pharaoh will offer a deal to trade our rights, freedom, sovereignty, and our Constitution for food and a bed at camp FEMA *(3 hots and a cot)*.

Heb 12:16 (NIV) See that no one is sexually immoral, or is godless like Esau, who for a single meal sold his inheritance rights as the oldest son.

When the Dollar fails and the world no longer wants Dollars, America will be helpless to print and spend for the people who are currently enjoying fiat government benefits. The federal level of services will probably be the last to fall because they will continue to print worthless Dollars to pay for their community programs. But the first to fall will be city, county, and state government programs. These states don't have the ability to print and spend. They must live within their budgets, and when those budgets collapse, America will literally descend into the horrors of the third world. Police, fire, and basic services will be reduced. Our roads and highways will not be repaired. Water, electric, trash removal, and other basic utilities will descend into third world repair status, and it might take weeks to get basic services installed or repaired. Trash pickup may be reduced to once per week or less. City offices will be reduced or closed, and things will slow down and become very dysfunctional. Abandoned homes and tall weeds in nice neighborhoods will become the norm. Policies, code enforcement, and menial upkeep will become last priority among city governments. Teachers will be laid off and good schools will be hard to find. Hospitals will shut down, and emergency rooms may require wait times of 8 – 12 hours before a person can see a doctor. These scenarios will probably get much worse as America "RESETS". This will be very painful, and many people will suffer and die as a result. Some will starve. Some will be victims of vicious crime, and others will be killed as they are committing crimes to try to feed their families. Still others will be indefinitely detained, imprisoned, or will die in fire fights against military or police forces. Utter chaos and an uncontrolled national environment could make survival a very hard thing for Americans for a season of time. This is very serious and not a scenario to be taken lightly.

During this season of crisis, Communism will make its move for totalitarian take over in America by painting a new world vision, and offering false hope to a weary, beaten down, and confused people who have no relationship with God, and no moral standards to live and die by.

"We Communists are like seeds and the people are like the soil. Wherever we go, we must unite with the people, take root and blossom among them"

- Mao Tse-Tung

Once the smoke clears, Washington's promises will have been broken; Americans will be impoverished, and a new financial and political leadership system will be thrust upon the people living in darkness, confusion, danger and chaos. The people will potentially act like Esau and trade their birthright for a meal and promise. National sovereignty would then die as the Constitution is forever suspended, and a Communist police state of martial law would wrap its tentacles around a beaten down, tired, and humbled population.

What is martial law and how do you get out of martial law and back to your Constitution after martial law is enacted? The short answer is, "You don't come out of it!"

Martial law is enacted when the commander in chief takes dictatorial command of the nation and he uses his military strength to enforce absolute control and obedience in the nation. This is normally done during times of a national crisis, a time of chaos, or a time of civil unrest, war, or civil war. It's very clear that America is set for martial law, and is actually under soft martial law at this time. The signing of NDAA on Dec. 31, 2011 brought America under martial law and suspended the Constitution. It's a done deal, but most people don't realize this. They will have a wake up call in the near future.

With current presidential orders in place, America doesn't need a national emergency for the president to declare open, hard core martial law. He can now just enact it at will, and suspend Congress and the Supreme Court at any time he feels he wants the power. This is very dangerous, very unconstitutional, and we are at this point "on purpose". Whose purpose? That's a great question, and one that you and I should have the answers to before going to bed TONIGHT!

How do you come out of martial law? The answer is that you don't. Martial law will most likely stay in place until a military coo or a long term collapse and failure of the Communist financial and political regime. This could take decades. Don't hold your breath and expect a "McDonalds drive through" quick answer once martial law is publicly enacted.

When peace settles in again after the national threat subsides, the dictator in chief has no reason to relinquish his newfound, unlimited powers along with the military leaders who enjoy absolute power. Just as Homeland Security was formed to fight the Jihadist Terrorists in the Middle East, it remains in place 10 years later, and is stronger and now turning its war inward towards those who live in the homeland. The suspension of our Constitutional rights after 9/11 have not been given back, because governments don't give freedom back once they have taken it, PERIOD! Take strong note of this. Soft martial law is in place now. What does this mean for your future in America? Will the government annul NDAA martial law? Only under a Ron Paul styled constitutional president and Congress. But the bulk of Americans are so far away from this mentality, and will not "Head West" until the announcement of Communism is made . . .

America as you have known it has ceased to exist,
All property lines have been dissolved,
And the U.S. Dollar is worthless."

- Quote from Dream #1, Scene #1

123

Congress is currently standing in the way of the Communist regime, and is purposely divided and showing itself to be useless. The Supreme Court is only an overseer of an old, outdated, antiquated Constitution *(in Communist – Socialist viewpoints)*, and the president would be forced to relinquish ultimate, dictatorial power if he allowed a re-establishing of the Constitution. This will not happen in almost all cases. The historical answer is that a nation DOES NOT come out from martial law.

America hangs by a thread. We are deep under water and going sideways in a cave and there is no way back to the surface without turning around immediately. Washington is not looking to get us out of the cave and back to the surface. They are looking for a deep, dark tunnel to enter and explore. The coming earthquake will forever trap Washington, "we the people", and the old system that has been dragged under by the deceptive doctrine of debt.

Prayer: *God, please help us all! Please renew the American eagle for one more round of flight. Give Samson one more act of strength to help bring freedom to the world and destroy the enemy armies that are threatening the world with evil intentions and death.*

Chapter 10
Decision Time: Hard Choices and Inconvenient Movements

Stalinism:

The communistic theories and practices developed by Joseph Stalin from Marxism and Leninism, especially his development of the cult of the individual with himself at its center, his advocacy of national revolution, and his extensive use of secret police and slave-labor camps to reduce opposition.

My mother had been educated at a convent, and she had been converted to communism by my father during Stalin's most rampant period, at the beginning of the 1930s. So she had two gods, God in heaven and god on earth.

- Guillermo Cabrera Infante

If you have read my dreams and believe them, you are now faced with some seriously hard choices. Whether you are an American, a U.S. Citizen, a resident in America, or even if you live internationally in another country, many of these next choices may end up being "life and death" decisions. They will become "prosperity or poverty" decisions and "fight or flight" decisions. I wish that none of us were in this predicament. However, the dream is unfolding at an unprecedented rate of speed and I believe that the time is upon us.

The good news is that God loves you and He will provide a way for you to escape if or when needed. But as it's been said to me before, "Son/daughter, you'd better NOT be late!".

There are always three groups of people in these time frames, such as in NAZI Germany and other hostile take over nations:

1. Those who get out with their finances.

2. Those who get out with their clothes on their backs.

3. Those who don't get out.

Likewise, there were different people in the Bible who got out at various stages.

1. Noah, who had a huge warning, decades ahead of the devastating flood, and who had time to build an ark of safety and provision.

2. Moses' mother, who sent him down the river in a dire emergency as the children in town were being slaughtered by Pharaoh's swords.

3. Jesus, whose parents were warned in a dream to flee immediately as Herod's sword was coming down upon the town to kill all children two years and younger.

4. Abraham found out ahead of time that God was planning to destroy Sodom (Genesis 18). However, Lot was told to leave immediately and don't look back in order to escape Sodom's destruction.

5. Jerusalem, at 70 AD who didn't get out because they didn't heed the warnings of God, and they defiantly stood in false pride as the Roman army besieged them, killing most of them and enslaving the rest while utterly destroying their city.

Each of these Bible characters fit into one of the three categories. Now, let me speak to you from position number one and let's use Noah's example as a secret biblical template to help you protect your family, faith, future, and finances.

When God revealed to Noah what was coming, He gave him a blueprint of what to build. If Noah would have taken a year off he would have drowned and humanity would have been lost. Don't be too confident that God will wait around for you if you are indecisive or want to start preparations next year. Get to task now and don't delay!

You must plan for the future that you believe is coming, no matter what that future actually ends up being like. To fail to plan is to seal your doom. Every government, every legitimate business, every military and every functioning organization has contingency plans. You must have contingencies too. Get your plans together, put a timeline of execution together, and get busy. "Son/daughter, don't be late!"

Hab 2:2-3 (NIV) **2** *Then the* LORD *replied: "Write down the revelation and make it plain on tablets so that a herald may run with it.* **3** *For the revelation awaits an appointed time; it speaks of the end and will not prove false. Though it linger, wait for it; it will certainly come and will not delay.*

Prov 15:22 (NIV) **22** *Plans fail for lack of counsel, but with many advisers they succeed.*

I am training clients on how to "BUILD AN ARK" based on Genesis 6. You can join that student group at **www.doctordanieldaves.com** . You need a container that will float through the coming storm. It must house your family and all of your seed bearing animals, as well as a store of food and supply for a designated period of time. You need three levels of protection for living, as well as a side door and a window in the top of your ark. If you get it built before the time comes for financial collapse, God Himself will shut you inside as he did Noah. He will close the door, and hide you inside your ark. I recommend that you start building yesterday.

You will need to find out who in your family is with you. And then together with them you must answer some serious questions like these:

1. Do I get out of the U.S.A. or do I stay while this thing unfolds?

2. If I get out of the U.S.A., which way do I go?

3. Do I have an emergency plan to get over one or more of the U.S. borders in case of a horrific event? Can I legally get out of America and into the contingent country?

4. How much will it cost to get out, where do I go, how will I finance it, and how will I make money once I'm gone?

5. What is my full checklist of things to do, paperwork to retrieve and things that I will need in the future? Passports? Bank

accounts? Retirement accounts? Seed start up money? Savings? Where do I go and blossom as a productive member of society?

6. Do I get out of debt, sell the house (while it's still mine), get out of the Dollar, buy hard assets, and cash in my IRA or 401k?

7. If I plan on staying in the U.S., do I move out of the heavily populated cities to stay away from riots and mass meltdown of insane society? Do I have friends somewhere that I can count on in times that I need to "bug out"?

8. Do I own firearms, have plenty of ammunition and loaded clips, fire proof safes and deep hiding places for valuables? Is my home secure from increased levels of violence in my neighborhood? Do I have a CHL license and understand the laws of my state concerning the use of firearms in crisis?

9. Have I considered the day that martial law is recognized and I am required to turn in my weapons of defense, ammunition, food storage, etc., effectively making myself and my family vulnerable to attack from anyone?

10. Do I have a contingency plan in case something really bad happens in my neighborhood or city? Can I get out?

11. What if the power grid is shut down and I suddenly have no electricity and/or the water shuts off at my tap? What if it became so dangerous for a period of time that I couldn't safely get to a grocery store? Or what if the shelves were stripped bare and a crisis destroyed the fragile North American food supply chain? Can I feed my family for a week? A month? A year?

12. If the U.S. Dollar fails, gas goes to $8 per gallon, the EPA seizes control of my home, or if I suddenly lose my property due to a new UN treaty, what are my plans? How much of my property and wealth am I willing to part with in order to secure my family's safety?

13. If I lose my job, what do I do next? Where do I go? Is my job on shaky ground? Is my industry on the way out of America? Do I need to secure different work? Do I need more multiple streams of income? Do I need different education? Do I need to look for a job outside of America before millions shoot past me looking for the same international jobs?

14. If martial law were to be announced with federal troops pouring into America's streets, would I be prepared if they locked down the borders and would not let me "out"? What if the government cancelled my passport? What if other "ticked off" nations would not allow Americans into their nations while hostilities were in play? What if I, my neighbors, or family members were targeted for detention and re-education? Am I spiritually, mentally, and physically prepared?

15. Do I have the legal documentation to get out of America? If the borders lock down, will Mexico let me into their country without residency status or a second passport? Can I get a second passport and how would I go about doing it?

If you live in another country other than the U.S., you are not out of the woods. You must answer your own set of questions, including:

1. What will a failed U.S. Dollar to do my nation's currency? Is my nation's currency a FIAT currency? Is it connected to the Dollar in any way? If so, will my country's government keep their currency connected to the Dollar? Will the people suffer devaluation in my country also, or will they let the currency unpin and strengthen when the Dollar fails? Will the people in my country revolt, rebel, and look for Americans to lynch?

2. Is my nation deeply connected to Western world commerce, and would a U.S. hostile take over or depression dramatically affect my nation, my job, and my property values? If so, how can I protect myself from this?

3. If a "one world" event seized control of the U.S., what powers might emerge in or around my country? For instance, would communists invade my nation knowing that the U.S. would not be intervening? And if that invasion were to occur, what would that mean for my family, job, business, assets, investments, etc.? Do I have a plan of escape?

4. Are there any financial bubbles in my nation that would pop if the U.S. went into a depression? If so, am I safe and can I prepare to purchase properties, businesses, and items at a deep discount after the bubble pops and prices reset?

5. If the U.S. cancelled my passport for any reason, and if they called me home as Nazi Germany did, as Communist Soviet Union did, etc., do I have a legal way that I can stay away from the U.S.? Do I have permanent residency status somewhere or a second passport?

I have a few ways to try to help you. I have dedicated my life to helping others who need a hand. Therefore, I'm always introducing new educational materials, emergency webinars, providing interviews on my radio programs, and getting you access to solid, newsworthy information to help you make critical decisions, build your ark of safety, stay in Psalm 91 protection, and live a life as worry free as possible while the systems of the world shake and quake.

1. I have up to date EMERGENCY FINANCIAL SEMINARS recorded for you which can be streamed 24/7 over the web. They will give you answers to the questions you are going to have. While I can't answer your questions for you, I can point you towards facts that can help you decide for yourself and your family. You can find the seminar at www.doctordanieldaves.com

   .

2. Contact me at info@doctordanieldaves.com and I will send you a full FREE list of 100 items to disappear off the store shelves in a crisis.

3. I have a one year mentoring program to help you identify and understand the giants in the marketplace, in government, in industry and wherever big money moves. You can ride into profit with them by finding where they are secretly going. I highly recommend this program. It's not cheap, but it includes everything that I have available in education, including four years of bi-weekly market training and education classes.

4. I have a monthly GIANT TRACKER REPORT which gives real time updates to the crisis or investment cycles at hand. If you

don't have time to be mentored or to research what's going on in your world, this report will give you key information regarding key movements of markets, industries, governments and the big money. I also discuss the state of the union and how to build your ark of safety in each monthly report.

5. Lastly, I recommend that you sign up FREE for our www.basicsforsuccess.ning.com investment community where I post blogs and support information multiple times per week.

Chapter 11
Private Final Thoughts to Help You Protect Yourself

Maoism:

The political and social theories and policies of Mao Zedong (1893-1976), Chinese communist leader, especially with regard to revolution and agrarian reform. Adherence to or belief in Mao's doctrines.

Socialism is simply Communism for people without the testosterone to man the barricades.

- Gary North

First and foremost, I believe that every Christian needs to make a divine connection with God and ask Him for divine direction concerning family, finances, and future. If you can get into the secret place of Almighty God (Psalms 91 protection), then no matter where you are on the planet, you can trust in His divine protection, supernatural open doors and miraculous supply and provision. No matter what comes to town, you can rest knowing that you are right where God wants you. There is no greater security than this. God has a place and a plan for each of His children, and this is the time for you to find your place and stick there. Being right where God wants you will make up for years of preparation and entrenchment that other Americans may try for survival.

Matt 6:25-34 (NIV) *25* *"Therefore I tell you, do not worry about your life, what you will eat or drink; or about your body, what you will wear. Is not life more important than food, and the body more important than clothes? 26 Look at the birds of the air; they do not sow or reap or store away in barns, and yet your heavenly Father feeds them. Are you not much more valuable than they? 27 Who of you by worrying can add a single hour to his life ? 28 "And why do you worry about clothes? See how the lilies of the field grow. They do not labor or spin. 29 Yet I tell you that not even Solomon in all his splendor was dressed like one of these. 30 If that is how God clothes the grass of the field, which is here today and tomorrow is thrown into the fire, will he not much more clothe you, O you of little faith? 31 So do not worry, saying, 'What shall we eat?' or 'What shall we drink?' or 'What shall we wear?' 32 For the pagans run after all these things, and your heavenly Father knows that you need them. 33 But seek first his kingdom and his righteousness, and all these things will be given to you as well. 34 Therefore do not worry about tomorrow, for tomorrow will worry about itself. Each day has enough trouble of its own.*

One man will work his entire, godless life to entrench himself, gain supplies, provision and try to prepare for a future event. Another man who seeks the Kingdom and God's righteousness first will receive a plan and the provision for the plan by God. It will come much easier than the godless worldling who must do it all on his own. I'm not minimizing the need to plan and prepare. But if you seek God's kingdom first, the plan and provision will be GIVEN and it will be the correct plan with correct provision for your true, long term future.

LEARN TO HEAR GOD'S VOICE:

I encourage you to get to a place where you can hear God's voice personally. There are many books and educational materials that will help you to hear God's voice on a personal, relational level and this ability is important. The Holy Spirit wants to give you daily direction and there are times in our lives when He will speak for us to move immediately and without delay. If Joseph didn't hear God in a dream, and if Noah didn't hear God's voice, we would not be here today. Prepare, practice, and learn to hear God's directional voice for yourself and your family.

WHERE SHOULD A PERSON LIVE:

People ask me where I believe they should live, and whether I think they should get out of America until the future is clear for "Terra America". I can't give anyone the answer that only God should give. But I do want to open the minds of believers everywhere and cause them to realize that there are bright locations all over the world for people to live which can be very fulfilling. If the dream was true that "All property lines have been dissolved", then there should be no property lines, boundaries, national borders, financial boundaries or any other line that holds you back from pursuing your future and destiny. If you choose to live in another country for a few years, I would applaud you. If you have children and your family can agree on moving, I would stand up and shout. Teaching your children another culture, another language, and dissolving their assumed boundaries will help accelerate them in the job and business markets of the world once they grow up. For a child to be able to learn like this would put them at the front of the line when it comes to international opportunities, high paying jobs, and bi-lingual capacities. And it wouldn't be wrong for you to learn another language for your future prosperity. Chinese is on the rise. Spanish will be the number one language in the world in just a few years. One day soon you will call a business and the operator will say, "For Spanish, press one". Are you ready for this encounter? Will your children be ready when bi or tri-lingual capacity will be the standard requirement for good jobs? I can take you to corporate managers right now who will hire a high school graduate who can speak two languages rather than a college grad with a $100,000 student loan and an "English only" language skill!

CAN I AFFORD TO LIVE OUTSIDE OF AMERICA?

People worry about being able to make the same amount of money in another nation. But you must realize that everything changes when you get outside of the U.S.A. Living in Central America, I have found that I can live on 40% of my U.S.A. income demands, and I can have a gardener and a maid as well. The food is organic, it's cheap and bountiful. I like to live where America's foods are grown and sent to America. There's no food shortage here. Housing is cheaper, utilities are cheaper, and there's no need for heaters or air conditioners where I like to live. Imagine it being 60 – 80 degrees year around. My unlocked iPhone works with unlimited internet for $22 per month. My mountain fresh water bill is $27 per year. Medical care is better than in the U.S. and it's about 10% - 20% of the cost in the U.S. Health insurance is pennies on the Dollar compared to medical insurance costs in the U.S. As of the writing of this book, the U.S. government will actually pay you to leave the country, giving you up to $92,500 of income tax free (per adult) each year (certain rules apply).

The rules and regulations for living are much more relaxed. It's just easier to live and work in many other countries, so you don't have to make as much money as you do in the high tax, high consumption, bubble society of debt dependency. While each nation has its own set of problems and hurdles, a change of pace can be very refreshing and a great family learning experience. Many people who make the move will never return to the U.S.A. because it's too restrictive, not free and there's too much waste. You might never come back if you find the right place in the world for your family to make a move.

Wouldn't it be great to become a family that travels the world while buying properties, establishing businesses, and making friends all over the world? All property lines have been dissolved, so you might as well get outside of your old borders and see what glorious opportunities await you out there.

WHAT ABOUT MY BUDGET?

I personally believe that Americans stand a strong chance of waking up one morning to a 30% - 50% devaluation of the U.S. Dollar value. It happens like clockwork when a currency is in its final death throes. Mexico experienced a 40%+ devaluation of the Peso in December 1994, and Mexicans woke up 40% poorer overnight. Zimbabwe announced a 90% devaluation overnight in 2009. I believe this is coming to America. Therefore, I strongly urge anyone who believes in the accuracy of the dream to consider making an emergency transition with your current budget. This is the season for prudent men to take hard line action ahead of an overnight devaluation, bank holiday and forced re-organization of Americas quickly lost wealth.

This means that a person needs to cut their budget by 50% immediately. I did whatever I needed to prepare for a Dollar that's worth 50% less than it is today. If a person fails to re-arrange their budget and the Dollar devalues against them, they will be in the throes of poverty with millions of Americans who also failed to prepare.

A person may need to sell their house and downsize to a smaller, cheaper rental home. They may need to get out of an existing auto loan and buy cars that are paid off. A great theme is to get out of debt and owe no man anything except God's love. If a person must, cut the cable bill, extra cell phone bills, and any fluff that's in the current budget. Drop the budget by at least 50% so an overnight devaluation won't have an effect. A person needs to take the extra 50% that is made each month and start banking it into hard assets, gold, silver, palladium, platinum, seeds, guns, ammo, food, fresh water filters and anything else that a family may need to get through some very hard times. As I mentioned in other areas of this book, a person should have some cash in hand to pay bills during a bank holiday, and extra seed money for amazing deals that will come available when unprepared Americans need to trade their hard assets for food, gas and other consumables. Remember the education from the dream, scene two?

A person needs to consider going through the garage and closets, and selling everything that's extra while there are still unsuspecting buyers with money in their hands. The day is potentially coming where these people will be reduced to impoverished paupers and there will be very few around who can buy "stuff". I personally want to be lean, mean and mobile during this season.

If or when an overnight devaluation of the Dollar comes, Americans will find that they are 50% poorer overnight. They will be caught in the middle of house and auto loans. They will be 100% spenders of what they earn on their current lifestyle. They will be forced by emergency survival to drop 50% of their living expenses as hyper inflation hits, food and gas prices double, recession and depression hit, jobs disappear, fear and panic hit nationwide, and the death cycle starts for the old American system of fiat.

"Name me a nation in history that has prospered by devaluing it's currency. There is nothing more insidious that a government can do to its people than to debase its currency."

- Rep. Paul Ryan

WHERE DO I INVEST?

Concerning investments, I cannot advise you on what to do because I'm not a licensed investment advisor. I must tell you to seek professional advice from your licensed broker or investment professional. However, I can tell you what I'm doing, or what I would do "IF" I had certain investments.

The U.S. Dollar. I am not interested in having a lot of Dollars under my long term care. As the Dollar finalizes its decline to $0 value, people who save Dollars will be losers. Their hard work saved in Dollars will turn to toilet paper. That's not a game I'm interested in playing.

Therefore, I am always looking to put some of my assets into the best currencies in the world that represent sanity in government and fiscal restraint. Some of those currencies at this time seem to be Canadian, Australian, Brazilian, and even South African over the Dollar.

I also like gold, silver, platinum, palladium, and other precious metals because God likes them. He built His temple and tabernacle out of these materials, and He told the Israelites to store up on them before He whacked Pharaoh. They are a true storehouse of wealth in a day when toilet paper Dollars are going to be tested by fire. Gold and silver are manipulated and kept low, but this is an extreme advantage for those of us who can see gold at a potential $5,000 - $10,000 per ounce, and silver potentially at $200 per ounce. When the uncontrollable death throes of the Dollar hit, these precious metals should go to the moon! In Germany at the end of the great collapse of their German Mark in 1919-1923, a person could buy an entire city block of commercial property with one ounce of gold! How many ounces did you say you wanted? Join the 5% club by getting gold and silver. 95% of Americans have none, YET!

I think that I should have access to six months of cash outside of my bank account, whether it's Dollars or other currencies, because I believe that there's a strong potential for a bank holiday. This would be a period of time where banks close, the currency is devalued and Americans become much poorer overnight. When the banks close, there will be no buying or selling unless you have cash in hand. It could be a very fearful and tight time for Americans who are unprepared. If I am correctly prepared, it could be a time to gather supplies and provisions for pennies on the Dollar as unprepared people throw their hard assets at me in exchange for some toilet paper called U.S. Dollars so they can pay bills, buy food, or meet the demands of the banker. The money that I have out of the bank in cash can also be "non loss" currency if I have a bank loan for a car or home. If the Dollar drops by 40% in an over night devaluation, and I have cash in my hands, I can use that cash to pay my car or home loan. This means that those Dollars did not devalue. Any other Dollars or cash equivalent could be valuable in trading for hard assets. Remember the man at the gas station? Someone might be willing to trade you a tractor for a few hundred bucks in cash. There is a reason that pawn shops are all over America. People have been trained to trade hard assets for consumables!

I think a devaluation could come at any time, and it could be 20% – 50%. One of the last major forced devaluations of the Dollar was 40% when gold was confiscated. It's happened before. Because the fed has printed so many $$$ Trillions, the devaluation must happen. It's actually already happened. The devaluation happens when they print. The physical effects of the devaluation are about to show up on main street. It will be great for the rogue elements of the federal government, because their debt will be written down by 20% - 50% with a stroke of the pen. But it will be at the total impoverishing of Americans who must pay the bill by losing the value of their life's savings.

One of the little things that I believe in is having six months of food stocked at home. *(Check current hoarding laws as they are changing to NOT allow you to store food.)* If there was ever a catastrophic event of any kind, I will want food on hand. And for the first time in my life, it's a better investment to put my money into food rather than leaving it in a savings account. Food prices rose as high as 28% last year, but interest rates on savings accounts are at 0%. Therefore, I made more money buying and storing food (which is a hard asset) than if I kept my money in the bank. It's easy to store food. I don't want bad tasting powdered foods that soldiers eat. I want to stock up on the stuff that I like to eat. If I like green beans then I should have six months of green beans on hand. I should have a system of rotation, bringing the older cans to the front and refilling with new cans at the back. This way, all of my foods stay fresh and in date and when I need that extra supply, it's food that I like to eat. Also, if I buy the beans for $.50 per can today and food goes up by 15% this year, I just saved a lot of money on my stored food supplies!

Of course, if a person moves to a food producing export country, there will be no food shortages when disaster strikes. If America's fragile food supply locks down, there will be mass quantities of food rotting on the docks of Columbia, Panama, Costa Rica, Honduras, Nicaragua, and Guatemala. They will be selling it to the locals for pennies on the Dollar because it will be in such plentiful supply.

WHAT ABOUT INTERNATIONAL BANKING?

I believe very strongly in getting money out of the country in an emergency fund. There are many reasons. First, a U.S. Citizen is not allowed to open bank accounts in a lot of other countries because of our oppressive government who threatens international banks with heavy fines, sanctions, and penalties when dealing with U.S. Citizens. Many banks just don't want the hassle, and they will turn you away if you request opening a bank account with a U.S. Passport. The problem is getting worse. In the coming months or years, you might not be allowed to open a bank account outside of the U.S.A. Does that sound like freedom to you?

Capital controls are coming in the United States that will restrict you from taking cash, belongings, currency, gold, silver, or property out of the U.S. You've heard of the form on the airplane that demands disclosure if you are transporting more than $10,000 out of the country? Well, it's going to get a lot worse, and U.S. Citizens will shortly be stopped from taking assets out of the U.S. by law and IRS policy. As of January 2013, you will be forced to prove that taxes have been paid on any funds that you want to take out of the country. If you can't prove that (how will you do that?) then the bank will be under compulsory threat to seize 30% of your transfer and give it to the IRS. You can then fight with the IRS to see if you ever get it back. Certain other laws are interwoven through the "Jobs Bill" and Obamacare which will stop your assets at the border. You may leave on vacation, but you must leave your assets behind. Check the history books on Nazi Germany if you want a living scenario of where those laws are potentially headed.

Remember an old familiar song from the Eagles . . . *"Welcome to the Hotel California, you can check out any time you'd like, but you can never leave."*

Some people tell me that they're afraid of putting their money in a foreign bank and they like the F.D.I.C. insurance that is offered to them in the U.S. My response is "Hogwash!". F.D.I.C. is bankrupt and under water. They are getting Federal Reserve bailouts just to stay afloat. Their insurance policy states that they promise to pay you back within

144

100 years if your bank defaults. In the event of a true collapse, your great grand children will receive a devalued life savings check that they can cash in for a McDonalds happy meal in 100 years. Foreign banks are in better shape than U.S. banks in my opinion, because they don't give 95%, 100% and 120% loans on properties. They don't have the luxury of Federal Reserve unlimited printing and bailouts. They need to operate in true banking principles. They require their clients to come up with a huge portion of the loan before they get involved. This keeps them safe and solvent. I like foreign banks myself. And there are some which pay me 6% – 10% just to keep my money with them.

If all hell broke loose in America or WWIII threatened to take the U.S. off the map with global thermo-nuclear war, I need a place of retreat for an extended vacation where I can read the paper, sip on some organic coffee, do some international business, and see how the future unfolds. I will do the Kingdom of God no good by being led to the slaughter with the simple, sinful, blind, deaf and ignorant. I plan to live another day to make maximum effect in the world for God. Therefore, I need a plan, a nation, and a bank account to help me pay for expenses when I'm on an extended emergency vacation. I will need an international bank account for that time. Don't expect your U.S. credit cards to work if there's a U.S. bank holiday. And you won't be taking $25,000 with you on the airplane. New capital controls are coming that will potentially limit us to less than $2,500. Why? Great question.

Remember that having a bank account outside the U.S. is currently legal. However, if I have certain amounts in the bank, I will be required to report that money to the IRS through certain forms filed with my annual taxes. If you have international accounts, make sure that you tell your tax preparer where your accounts are so you don't forfeit the account in its entirety to the IRS.

If I EVER plan to do business in other countries, or if I ever plan on creating an income internationally, I am going to need bank accounts. Now is the time to make friends with foreign bankers, get bank accounts opened, start a foreign corporation and get authority in place so I can move freely, start a business, produce gainful employment, etc. In the day of disaster, the simple will be in absolute turmoil. Don't be among the simple during that day. God will laugh at the simple.

Prov 1:22-33 (NIV) "How long will you simple ones love your simple ways? How long will mockers delight in mockery and fools hate knowledge? If you had responded to my rebuke, I would have poured out my heart to you and made my thoughts known to you. But since you rejected me when I called and no one gave heed when I stretched out my hand, since you ignored all my advice and would not accept my rebuke, I in turn will laugh at your disaster; I will mock when calamity overtakes you-- when calamity overtakes you like a storm, when disaster sweeps over you like a whirlwind, when distress and trouble overwhelm you. "Then they will call to me but I will not answer; they will look for me but will not find me. Since they hated knowledge and did not choose to fear the Lord, since they would not accept my advice and spurned my rebuke, they will eat the fruit of their ways and be filled with the fruit of their schemes. For the waywardness of the simple will kill them, and the complacency of fools will destroy them; but whoever listens to me will live in safety and be at ease, without fear of harm."

WHAT ABOUT MY RETIREMENT PLAN?

If I have an IRA or 401k, I need to gain absolute control of that retirement account. I will not allow my company or any investment firm to lie to me and tell me that I cannot have control over my retirement. I either need to exit that plan and take the 30% tax hit, or I need to position the retirement account outside of the Federal government's direct control. I could buy property in a foreign nation. Maybe a piece of land or a rental property. This would tie the funds up where they can't be confiscated to fill the empty coughers of Social Security (which is in the works). I could buy physical gold or silver, or I could buy into gold and silver companies through a stock brokerage account so my retirement will go up when the Dollar declines into the pit to $0. Of course, those funds could be confiscated by the Federal government if they wave their magic wand and commandeer those funds into their hands. If I still have some time before my retirement, I should consider protecting these retirement funds from a hostile Dollar and a rogue government. Remember, I am not telling you what to do, but giving you insight into my thoughts for my own retirement plan.

I have a friend who took his IRA out, paid the 30% penalty, and bought gold at $300 per ounce. His wife thought he was crazy. However, he was just informed while everyone else slept. He and his wife are very happy now, knowing where gold and silver have risen to. If I believe the Dollar is going to $0 value before I retire, it would be worth taking the 30% penalty hit to secure the retirement funds into physical gold, silver, or hard assets. At least those assets will still be worth something when I retire. If I continue to hold Dollars, I will look at a pile of worthless toilet paper while I forget any retirement in my lifetime. If we wake up one morning to a 40% devaluation of the Dollar, I will have missed my opportunity to opt out with only a 30% penalty instead of the newly imposed 40% devaluation.

WHAT ABOUT THE STOCK MARKET?

If I hold investments in the stock market, I should seek valuable wisdom from those who believe like I do. The stock market will be a slippery slope for most. Even if the market makes huge gains upwards during Dollar devaluation, I will be heavily taxed on all of those gains. Therefore, while I may have made 20% on a rocketing market, I may be giving 30% of those gains back to the government, while the value of my Dollar has dropped by 30%. Therefore, I could have lost money just by staying in the stock market.

KEEPING WHAT I HAVE FROM THE THIEVES:

This is a period of time which I believe will be different than any other time in our lifetime history. Through this long term reset of America, most Americans are looking for a place to put their investment funds where they can still make money during this tough period of downturn. It's a very hard thing for most to find winning investments at this time. But I believe that the real goal for most Americans needs to be to KEEP what you have rather than to make profits like the old days. The Bible gives me the cyclical clues in stories like Israel in Egypt, Noah and the ark, and survival through an earthquake or fire. My money can be hidden in Psalm 91 protection if I will invest it into God's economy.

Heb 12:26-29 (NIV) At that time his voice shook the earth, but now he has promised, "Once more I will shake not only the earth but also the heavens." The words "once more" indicate the removing of what can be shaken--that is, created things--so that what cannot be shaken may remain. Therefore, since we are receiving a kingdom that cannot be shaken, let us be thankful, and so worship God acceptably with reverence and awe, for our "God is a consuming fire."

WHAT ABOUT HOME OWNERSHIP?

As far as home ownership and rental property ownership, I have strong thoughts. I believe that the government is covertly planning on confiscating personal property through methods written earlier in this book. Therefore I think it's risky to own property in the U.S. right now. If you own a home and have any equity in that home, remember that the equity is not real or realized until you get the equity into your hands in hard cash. Otherwise, it's stated equity only, and is subject to housing prices and their swings. If my dream is true, then housing prices could plummet much farther than they have already. Who wants to buy a home in Communist America? Who has money left to buy a home at current prices if they lose 40% of their wealth in an overnight Dollar devaluation? And if energy prices, hyper inflation or other elements cripple our economy, another wave of foreclosures will thrust millions of homes on the market with no buyers, dropping home values once again. The dangers are so real that I don't want to own any property unless it's a rental that's bringing income, and it's paid off with no bank loan attached to it. And even then, that property is ripe for confiscation and will not survive if all property lines are dissolved in America through a hostile Communist take over.

WHAT ABOUT RENTAL PROPERTIES?

Concerning rental properties, the old standard business model for landlords was to get a loan for maximum amount possible (at the old price) and try to get into the home for no money down. Then the home becomes a positive cash flow business as the renter pays more in rent than the landlord owes to the bank each month. Hopefully that home makes $50 - $250 per month positive cash flow. This is the old business model in the old world. But watch what will happen when the new world economy runs up against this old business model.

I know many famous people who were saved from the first wave of financial collapse because rents didn't go down while property values did go down. One famous author owns thousands of homes, and those homes dropped as much as 50% in value. However, the rents have remained the same so he didn't lose the homes to the bank through inability to pay. It looks like this:

OLD WORLD TYPICAL RENTAL BUSINESS:

Old world 2007 rental home value:	$100,000
Bank loan on this home at 95%:	$ 95,000

(P.I.T.I.) Principle, Interest, Taxes, Insurance:	$ 900 Mo.
Rent Income:	$1,000 Mo.
Positive Cash flow:	$ 100 Mo.

The value of the home drops to $65,000 in the financial meltdown. However, rents stay the same, so although the home is upside down in value, the landlord can still make the payments as long as the renter continues to make the payment. All is well, until wave two hits.

NEW WORLD RENTAL HOME PROBLEMS COMING:

New world 2012 rental home value: $ 65,000
Bank loan on this home at 95%: $ 95,000
Home equity value is -$30,000.

Because of a wave of foreclosures in America, there are many new rental homes available at the lower $65,000 price. Investors have scooped up these homes at great discounts. Some have been picked up for $40,000 - $50,000 by multi-property buyers. Now, next door to the $900 rental home, a landlord has just picked up a rental home for $60,000.

New world, new landlord home bought: $60,000
Bank loan on this home at 95%: $57,000
Home equity is +$3,000
The next door old world property equity is -$38,000 when compared to the newly priced rental home.

(P.I.T.I.) Principle, Interest, Taxes, Insurance: $600   Mo.
Rent Income: $800   Mo.
Positive Cash flow: $200   Mo.

Here's the problem. The tenant paying $1,000 per month can now move next door into a comparable home for $200 savings per month. They can use that money to help fuel their $5 per gallon auto and buy their $5 bread, milk, and eggs. They head to the lower priced home. The old world home landlord CANNOT compete because he can't bring rents down to match the newly priced home. He makes $0 profit at $900 per month, and he loses money at $800 per month rent. Therefore, he must turn the keys into the bank and lose the home as a failed business investment. Equity will plummet on homes everywhere in that neighborhood, and rental prices could continue to drop in a deflationary cycle.

How do you survive this? The only way I know how to survive this onslaught will be to have my rental properties paid off in full. That way I can offer the lowest rent in the community and I can always compete with the landlord down the road. However, I must attempt to protect the equity in my rental property through legal entities, and I must be willing to lose the property to seizure if America falls to communism.

BUSINESS OWNERSHIP IN AMERICA?

If I own a business in America, I must make hard decisions to cut costs, cut waste, and streamline the business for tough times ahead. If I determine my business to be a "boutique fluff" business, and if I believe times are going to get much worse for Americans and their wealth, then I must consider selling or closing that business with the least impact as possible. I must begin to direct my business towards the hard core needs of Americans rather than their desires or wants. During tough depressions and recessions, people buy cheap food, cheap clothing, cheap autos, they repair their cars and homes themselves instead of hiring the jobs done, and they cut out all of the puff and fluff of the old "good times". I must at least get my business out of debt, build a buffer "rainy day" fund, and draw a hard and solid " Sorry, We've Closed Our Doors" line in the sand if the business goes into negative territory. I cannot allow false "hope and change" to cause me to hang on to a dead horse while it drains me of my savings and seed money. Decisions must be made now before it all hits the fan. Making reasonable decisions in the middle of the heat will not prove fruitful. I must buckle down, let employees go, cut back their hours, and make the business a lean and mean operating machine. If I feel that I can sell it before trouble comes, that is a serious option. If I can streamline the business so it can operate on its own with me living in another country on a smaller income, then I must take that into consideration.

If I must get into business during this season, I need to look at extremely great priced deals. I need to help an old world owner out of his pain by taking the weight off of his shoulders. But I should not buy anything at current world prices, because I know that the price is going to get better in the future. Therefore, anything I buy must have a buffer in place to protect me from price drops in the future. And my new business model needs to cater to the needs of broke Americans and those who can't live without my services. This will probably bring you to the industries of food, auto or handi-man repair, betterment education, security, money saving programs, devices and transportation, and cheap entertainment. There are probably more programs. I just need to think hard before making any long term commitments. The business must also survive a roll out of police state seizure or communism. It must also be able to convert out of a failed monetary system and into a new currency, or able to trade hard assets for services. I must remember that business rents may be going down drastically. Therefore I don't want to lock myself into a five year triple net lease rate, knowing that the bubble could pop and make my business non competitive in the new world.

PERSONAL FINANCIAL MOVEMENTS:

If I were to convert myself out of the old world before the masses are running in a panic, I would sell my home and move into a rental for a much better price than owning. I wouldn't be in the crosshairs of the EPA, green police, the Federal Reserve's desire for my home equity, and I wouldn't be on the long term hook for a home that I can't sell. I would set myself under a one to three year lease obligation with a 60 day exit clause which allows me optimum freedom to move as needed. I am totally mobile and portable. If rents decline in my area, I could try to re-negotiate a new price with my landlord, or move next door to a cheaper home.

PAY OFF, SAVE AND AMASS EMERGENCY WEALTH:

I would pay off every loan I have and start amassing wealth at an emergency rate of speed. I would seriously, seriously enter a plan of cutting back and saving. Most people say, "I can't afford to save." I say to them, "Then you will die with the rest of them." Wisdom calls for us to leave our simple ways and take action. Even God laughs at the simple when they despise a plan of action and get caught in calamity.

Seriously, if you found out that you had ten months to live unless you came up with the money to buy a surgery that would cost one year's worth of salary, I guarantee that you would have that salary in hand before the 10 months was up. You'd do anything possible to save your life. The problem is not that we don't have the ability, it's that we don't really believe enough in the future to act on it. Faith is action, and faith without action is dead. Therefore, the complaint that says, "I can't" doesn't fly with God, truth, or reality.

BECOMING LEAN AND MEAN:

While we sit in the eye of the hurricane and the weather is calm, I would sell everything that I don't need: extra phone, cable, the second car payment, and all the junk in the garage. Extras of everything that I have should be sold. I am becoming lean and mean. I'm preparing for movement and action. I'm getting my seed together for my future. I'm amassing gold, silver, precious stones, extra food, guns, ammo, and things that I can trade with and sell in tough times. I'm cutting the waste now at a higher price before I'm forced in the future at low discounted prices. I'm downsizing my home if at all possible. Instead of eating out three times per week, I'm banking the cash and eating out two times per month. I'm finding new ways to entertain myself and my family and I'm banking seed money. I'm taking this thing very seriously and I'm thanking God for another day of peace where I can trim down, sell the extra, and prepare for a very different world in the future.

I've considered whether or not I think my job would make it through a 50% unemployment rate in America. If I believe that it's gone, I'm already looking for a different job in a highly desired field, wherever on the planet it might take me. I will not wait to get in line with 5,000 other hungry people who are looking for the same job. I am pro-active, I am ahead of the curve, and I am protecting my future as a good Christian, a good husband, a good father, and a good man who leaves an inheritance rather than consuming that inheritance on myself. Whether or not the worst happens, I am prepared. I have discharged my duties before God and I have done all I can to protect my family, finances, and future. I trust God to complete the rest of the direction, protection, and provision.

Prov 13:22 (NIV) A good man leaves an inheritance for his children's children, but a sinner's wealth is stored up for the righteous.

WHAT TIMELINE DO WE HAVE BEFORE THE COLLAPSE ACCELERATES?

This is a great question. I don't have a time in mind, but only the season. And it's my opinion that we are in that season right now. I believe that time is very short, and every day that we have not collapsed into manifest depression is a gift from God to build the ark of safety! I believe that the first part of the hurricane has hit, and there will be a brief period of clear skies and good weather before the back side of the hurricane hits. This will be the most damaging and destructive in my opinion.

These are the warning signs that I'm looking for:

A.   Federal government preparing for a mass civil uprising because of the robbery and seditious movement coming upon the people by the world bank and elite interests. This preparation is already in place, as well as: laws, presidential orders, and military readiness.

B.   A crack and public exposure in the derivatives market which will start rocking the banking and currency world. The current Las Vegas styled derivatives bets that America's top nine banks are exposed to equals over $200 Trillion Dollars, which "we the people" are legally on the hook for. This does not include the national debt. These are just bad gambling debts that F.D.I.C. will be responsible for if these bets go wrong. When this market begins to crack publicly, the end of the Dollar is near. J.P. Morgan just cracked $2 Billion in derivatives bets gone bad. These are the cracks I'm looking for, and they're happening now.

C.   Currency wars and trade wars will become very public, as nations begin to position themselves to escape the falling Dollar. These currency wars are already beginning to appear in this season.

D.   When the Federal Reserve begins to raise interest rates, this is the end. Interest is the only tool left in their belt to try to hold the Dollar together. However, when they raise interest by 1%, this will increase the U.S. national deficit by $140 Billion per year. If the Federal Reserve raises interest by 10% in an emergency attempt to save the Dollar, the United States just added $1.4 Trillion per year to its bankrupt deficit, and in my opinion, the entire ship sinks like the Titanic. The last time the Federal Reserve had to raise interest rates to save the Dollar was in 1980 in an emergency. The interest rate went to 20%. Where will it go in this coming emergency?

WHAT IF I'M WRONG AND NOTHING HAPPENS?

If none of the things in my dream happen, if the U.S. government figures a way to pay off its insurmountable $200+ Trillion debt, if the laws of mathematics don't work this time around, and if the Dollar becomes strong despite man's destructive forces to purposely destroy it, then I have planned as a good soldier of Christ. I have cut back, trimmed the fat, and amassed a store of more savings than I ever imagine doing during any normal time. Period. I am more wealthy, I am mobile, and I am ready to invest into the new world that never failed or fell. I am in better shape than I would have been, and I have learned to always be prepared. I have taught my family well, and God is happy with my oversight of everything that He has entrusted into my care. I am a winner, and I understand what it is to protect and preserve that which God has given. I have trained my children to always be prepared and to always plan for the future.

If the dream is true, which I absolutely believe that it is, then I am ready for the storm. My ark of Psalm 91 safety is built, loaded, and stocked with enough provision to get me through the storm and onward to the other side. On that other side, a brand new world awaits for my family to plant seed under a rainbow of God's promise!

A WORD TO COMMUNITY, PUBLIC, CHURCH AND BUSINESS LEADERS:

We are being pushed into a biblical event which is going to require great strength, a love for the truth, and possibly the laying down of our lives for the sake of God, truth, and our fellow man. This is not a day to live at ease, but this is the season to train yourself, your people, and your leaders, for potential disasters and disruptions ahead.

I understand the need to remain positive, and to stay in faith. However, many of America's people are currently suffering from, or will suffer from NORMALCY BIAS. People all over America are saying, "Well,

158

it's all in the Lord's hands. We just need to trust God with the outcome." When you hear talk like this, you know most assuredly that they are suffering from the NORMALCY BIAS, and are sticking their heads in the sand in sheer panic and fear. The statement is one of trust, but the bias is one of mental stress.

*The **normalcy bias**, or normality bias, refers to a mental state people enter when facing a disaster. It causes people to underestimate both the possibility of a disaster occurring and its possible effects. This often results in situations where people fail to adequately prepare for a disaster, and on a larger scale, the failure of governments to include the populace in its disaster preparations. The assumption that is made in the case of the normalcy bias is that since a disaster never has occurred then it never will occur. It also results in the inability of people to cope with a disaster once it occurs. People with a normalcy bias have difficulties reacting to something they have not experienced before. People also tend to interpret warnings in the most optimistic way possible, seizing on any ambiguities to infer a less serious situation. (From Wikipedia.org)*

Leaders of truth are going to be forced into a new style of leadership in this coming season. We will not have the luxury of not speaking the truth because it might offend someone. We must prepare the people for critical times. We must also prepare them to reach into their communities, calm the fearful, feed the needy, and give solid direction when confusion abounds. Our job is not to just save "us four, no more" but to reach out to those who will be coming into our realm of influence. And I believe that they will be coming in droves, looking to follow solid leaders who are not afraid to lead in the new world.

This is a time to get your leaders together and begin making emergency plans for your homes, families, churches, and businesses. What can your leadership team do to help your community? Can you provide food, water, supplies, shelter, protection, and more in a crisis?

Are your people ready to move as a team? United we stand, divided we fall. No man will be a successful island to himself in the day of financial collapse and disaster. Your community leadership must be in place and ready to take action. It will be too late to make people aware and train them once the panic starts. People will not follow a person who is following the crisis. They will follow those who show strong leadership and who have taken action before the crisis.

As a leader, an American, a father, mother, pastor, or business owner, you may be forced to make a solid decision for freedom, justice, and liberty or stand by and watch a hostile communist take-over.

Our brethren are already in the field! Why stand we here idle? What is it that gentlemen wish? What would they have? Is life so dear, or peace so sweet, as to be purchased at the price of chains and slavery? Forbid it, Almighty God! I know not what course others may take; but as for me, give me liberty or give me death! - Patrick Henry 1775

These are words spoken from a man who was forced to make a decision. He didn't look for trouble. It came looking for him. His answer went down in history so that others can follow his lead with great courage.

If Communism attempts a hostile take-over of America, you and your people will need to be led by God. I cannot tell you what to do or how to do it. But I can stand with you and pray, "God bless my fellow brothers and sisters as we are willing to lay our lives down for our children's freedom, liberty, and peace.

I found a Federal law which is called "Misprision of Treason". This law commands every American, owing allegiance to the United States, to disclose any potential act of treason to the president, the governor or a judge. The consequence of not speaking out in defense of your nation and Constitution is a fine and/or imprisonment for seven years.

US FEDERAL LAW: 18 USC § 2382

MISPRISION OF TREASON: *Whoever, owing allegiance to the United States and having knowledge of the commission of any treason against them, conceals and does not, as soon as may be, disclose and make known the same to the President or to some judge of the United States, or to the governor or to some judge or justice of a particular State, is guilty of misprision of treason and shall be fined under this title or imprisoned not more than seven years, or both.*

It is a crime for you and I to remain silent if there is a possibility of treason taking place in America. If the watchman remains silent, the blood of innocent people will be on his hands. If you and I remain silent, we will be guilty before God and men of misprision of treason, or treason itself.

Joshua 24:15 And if it seem evil unto you to serve the LORD, choose you this day whom ye will serve; whether the gods which your fathers served that were on the other side of the flood, or the gods of the Amorites, in whose land ye dwell: but as for me and my house, we will serve the LORD.

Finally, I want to encourage you to stand for truth, justice, righteousness, and God's Kingdom in this final hour.

1 Cor 16:13-14 (NIV) Be on your guard; stand firm in the faith; be men of courage; be strong. Do everything in love.

Esth 4:14 (NIV) For if you remain silent at this time, relief and deliverance for the Jews will arise from another place, but you and your father's family will perish. And who knows but that you have come to royal position for such a time as this?"

God needs your presence, your voice, and your willingness to stand. He will open the doors and the hearts for you. He will insert you at the right time and place, to bring great world change through the greatest power of all, the power of love.

Chapter 12
A Final Prayer

Leninism:

The political doctrines of Vladimir llich Ulyanov (Lenin), founder of Bolshevism, architect of the current Soviet government, originator of the Comintern, and author of the imperative that the Soviets lead the proletariat of other nations to revolution and communism.

The goal of socialism is communism.

- Vladimir Lenin

I want to offer a final prayer for you, your family, our nation, and our world.

Heavenly Father, I come to you in the powerful name of your Son Jesus Christ, the savior of the world, the author of life, and the one who guides His own with provision, protection, and divine direction. I acknowledge You as the creator of the Heavens and the earth, and the founder of America and all nations. I know that Heaven is Your throne and the earth is Your footstool. I know that You rule over the nations and You appoint the kings, presidents, and rulers in all of the lands. You have a sovereign plan for the nations, and I pray that your plan would move forward without any further delay from hinderers, anti-christs or unbelievers.

Lord, I humbly ask you first of all to sovereignly watch over the United States of America and all of the nations of the world. Subdue, chain, and fetter wicked kings, rulers, and the sons of Belial who are purposely building the "one world" "globalist elite" beast system of control, slavery, and poverty to bind the innocent. Stop them cold in their tracks. May they fall into their own traps and be hung from their own gallows. May their wicked seed give them a harvest that will knock them out of power, influence, and authority. Bring Heaven's intervention as your people raise their voice in effective prayer for the salvation and healing of their lands. Cause a great return of human hearts towards your truth, your love, and to receive the powerful sacrificial gift of life through your Son Jesus.

I pray for my friends and family, and all who have read the dream and are taking heed to the revelation of the future. I ask Lord that you calm our hearts. Do not let our hearts be troubled. There are things that we must do in the natural to prepare for future events. These things can be taxing and stressful. But I ask that your Holy Spirit will guide us, keep us, and open supernatural doors of supply and provision so we can get everything on the checklist completed in record time.

I thank you for Heaven's light on our situations, and I ask you to speak directly to each of us "where" you want us to go, to live, to work, and to raise our families. Give us a successful five year, ten year, twenty year and fifty year attainable vision. Fill our hearts with wisdom, our minds with knowledge, and our eyes with vision. Give us eyes to see and ears to hear while the world walks in blindness and deafness. Give us eyes like the owl, who can see clearly during the darkness of night. He has the wisdom to know what is actually going on while the night creatures are on the move, feeding, hunting, and doing their "night work". Let us be like the owl who is also known as the "night eagle", and rest safely from our perch above.

I ask that you give us provision for today, and provision for the journey ahead. Provision for our families and for others who will need help along the way. Give us a building plan for an ark of safety just like you gave to Noah, and help us to complete it in time before the fires, floods, earthquakes, and storms hit the failed world system of fallen man. I call upon Psalm 91 divine protection for your children everywhere. Though 1000 may fall at our side and 10,000 at our right hand, it will not come to our door. We will not be afraid of catastrophes, wars, violence, or troubling events. We rest peacefully under your great wings of mighty protection and are safe. Ultimately, we are surrounded by your great love, angelic protection, and we are empowered to go "through" this time with success.

Thank you for giving your leaders wisdom and courage. I ask that you free and liberate humanity from the controlling forces of hell, the spirit of Pharaoh, and the plots of world rule by the sons of Belial. You are the King and Lord over all creation and we trust you for help during these days of darkness and disaster.

Lord, we are encompassed with a flood of ungodly men and women who have been sent by Satan to thwart your purposes and hinder the advancements of your Kingdom. According to David's prayer in Psalms, Judge these wicked men and sons of Belial, O God, and let the angel of the Lord chase them. May their ways be slippery and may they fall in their own ditches and traps that they have set for others. May they hang from their own gallows. Let their end come suddenly and without remedy. I know that you have promised that wicked people must pay for their transgressions. I pray for them to repent. If they repent Lord, turn their hearts from wickedness and towards the truth. Cleanse them of their wickedness by the blood of Jesus. I also pray Father that they either turn or burn, and that their wickedness on this earth would end according to your will. Then your people will be free to live in righteousness, liberty, and have the freedom to follow You according to Your Word and the dictates of their hearts.

Lord, I pray that you would turn Americans back to their roots, to the Lamb of God, to their Constitution, and to their destiny. Wake us up and open our eyes and ears to see the truth, to embrace the truth, and to fight for truth.

Thank you for hearing my prayer, and according to Matthew 18:19, I know that my prayer is being answered as two of us agree together in asking you for these things.

I pray all of these things in the mighty name of the only Lord, the only King, the author of life and salvation, my risen Lord and Savior Jesus Christ.

- The End

Stay Up To Date With National, International, Government & Market Movements With Dr. Daniel Daves

Subscribe To The "Giant Tracker™" Monthly Report Today!

www.gianttracker.com

Join The Christian Investment Community

To See Critical News Updates, Read Blogs By Dr. Daniel Daves, & Stay On The Right Side of The Markets.

Post Your Own Blogs, Comments, Photos & Videos. Make Friends & Learn Together. Sign Up Is FREE.

www.basicsforsuccess.ning.com

Christine LeGarde - ordered
The magic "7" - compress#'s
2014 drop 0 - 14 2 X 7

2014 - mile Stone magic

100th anniversary WWI
Bretton Woods anniversary
70 drop the zero
#25 -

FALL Berlin wall

7 miserable weak & fragile

IMF will have something to do
with it.

7 strong years - strength & might

Made in the USA
Charleston, SC
19 September 2013